Viktor Frankl and the Book of Job

Viktor Frankl and the Book of Job
A Search for Meaning

Marshall H. Lewis

Foreword by
Alexander Batthyány

James Clarke & Co

James Clarke & Co

P.O. Box 60
Cambridge
CB1 2NT
United Kingdom

www.jamesclarke.co
publishing@jamesclarke.co

Paperback ISBN: 978 0 227 17727 3
PDF ISBN: 978 0 227 90728 3

British Library Cataloguing in Publication Data
A record is available from the British Library

First published by James Clarke & Co, 2020
Copyright © Marshall H. Lewis, 2019

Published by arrangement
with Pickwick Publications

All rights reserved. No part of this edition may be reproduced, stored electronically or in any retrieval system, or transmitted in any form or by any means, electronic, mechanical, photocopying, recording, or otherwise, without prior written permission from the Publisher (permissions@jamesclarke.co).

Contents

List of Illustrations | v
Foreword by Alexander Batthyány | vii

1. The Terrible Paradox of Suffering | 1
2. Viktor Frankl's Logotherapy | 22
3. Logotherapy and Hermeneutics | 39
4. Job and Frankl's Existential Vacuum | 57
5. Job and Frankl's Will to Meaning | 82
6. Job and Frankl's Self-Transcendence | 103
7. The Eyes of a Child | 119

Bibliography | 125
Index | 131

Illustrations

Figure 1. Frankl's Dimensional Ontology | 30
Figure 2. Frankl's First Law of Dimensional Ontology | 32
Figure 3. Frankl's Second Law of Dimensional Ontology | 33

Foreword

ONE OF THE SIGNS of the maturation of a scientific discipline is its applicability in unexpected contexts; and one of the prime signs of both the intellectual curiosity and ability of a researcher is to actually engage his or her discipline and its methods in said unexpected context—and, importantly, succeed. This treatise on the Book of Job is a case in point. It connects two research traditions that so far rarely have been brought together, namely, hermeneutics on the one hand and a prominent branch of existential psychotherapy, logotherapy and existential analysis, on the other.

The outcome is an analysis of the Book of Job—next to Qoheleth arguably one of the most existential books of the Old Testament—that guides the reader through a passage towards a deep personal, existential, and historical understanding of the problem of unjustified suffering and the despair and doubt which can come with it, and yet does not end there, but continues until it reaches areas and insights that very few treatises of the Book of Job ever reach.

For at the end of the journey, and in hindsight, Job (and the reader) will look back and perhaps understand that what lies behind them is not a linear narrative, but an interactive structure in which subject and object, experience, understanding, and outer and inner happenings make for a complex web of events—far too complex to allow for simple and easy answers.

Hence, in contrast to theological attempts to understand (the God of) the Book of Job, this book analyzes its subject from a first-person (i.e., Job's) perspective; and yet in contrast to accounts primarily based on psychodynamic models of personhood, it does not solely focus on the subjective experience of Job (and the reader). Rather, it attempts to reconnect the self and the world. It thus attempts to fulfill what one of the early Austrian-American pioneers of existential and phenomenological psychiatry, Rudolf Allers, defined as the ultimate goal of all psychotherapy and philosophy: To

FOREWORD

reconcile man and the world by looking not only at what is (conditions), but also at that which could (freedom) and should (meaning) be.

This book, then, combines some of the core ideas of the personalist existentialist tradition, and in doing so allows for ambiguity where allowing ambiguity is due, and clarity where it is possible. And in contrast to the French existentialist tradition, it refrains from declaring to be "absurd" what on closer inspection merely turns out to allow for different, and sometimes contradicting, interpretations. Readers may look at figure 2 to get a preview on how the seemingly absurd or self-contradicting can either be a temptation to give up one step too early and claim that things that don't make sense are "absurd"—or an invitation to gain a deeper understanding of the nature of reality. This book, then, is such an invitation. It is an eye-opener.

Next to the fact that this book is an intellectual and scientific masterpiece and succeeds in establishing a new research methodology within the personalist existentialist tradition, there remains of course the open question of the relationship between providence and the problem of evil and suffering. Will we ever know THE answer to this problem? In all likelihood: No.

And yet, as the analysis of this book implies, the problem is perhaps not so much the unfound answer as it is the question. For inasmuch as impersonal meaning would be the designator of something so remote from everyday human existence that it would have little, if any, actual existential relevance, an impersonal, generic answer to the problem of suffering would also be far too removed from actual human experience to be of solace, or perhaps even understandable (which, by the way, also portrays Frankl's position on the theodicy problem: He held that there is indeed an answer, but one that we would not be able to understand intellectually). But, as this book shows, it is possible to address the problem of evil and suffering without fully understanding it; and the answer is not merely cognitive or affective, but existential.

This, then, is an outstanding testimony of the strength of the personalist existentialist approach to one of the core questions of the human condition; it is destined to become a classic both due to its original line of thought and the rarely found blend of sensitivity and knowledge so impressively present throughout its chapters.

Prof. Dr. Alexander Batthyány
The Endowed Viktor Frankl Chair for Philosophy and Psychology
Liechtenstein

1

The Terrible Paradox of Suffering

THIS BOOK WILL DEVELOP a hermeneutic based on the existential approach to suffering of Dr. Viktor E. Frankl. The process will first situate Frankl's logotherapy and existential analysis within the disciplines of psychology and hermeneutics. Frankl's therapeutic approach will be explored. This approach does not dictate a specific meaning for any given event, but consists of a set of psychological principles that allow for the discovery of personal meaning within any given event.[1] Frankl's indebtedness to existentialism and phenomenology will be explored.[2] Finally, Frankl's principles will be developed into a hermeneutic that will be applied to the Book of Job. A logotherapy hermeneutic is one that can provide a vocabulary to reveal truths discovered in the text. As a vocabulary closely associated with both meaning and suffering, it is in a unique position to do so; that is, it is in a unique position to read and understand the text. Special emphasis will be placed on the question of whether Job will "curse God and die." The question of disinterested piety, or whether Job "fears God for nothing," will be explored. Job's final, ambiguous response to the speeches of God will be treated as an existential challenge to the reader. The book will conclude with a discussion of how a logotherapy hermeneutic is of benefit in understanding and responding to this challenge.

The hermeneutic developed here may best be described as a postmodern reading of the book of Job falling within what David E. Klemm

1. Frankl, *The Will to Meaning*, 67.
2. Frankl, *The Will to Meaning*, 10.

describes as practical philosophy, "when interest shifts from the understood meaning to the activity of understanding."³ Klemm goes on to explain, however, that such a shift does not mean that one looses interest in the meaning presented by the text. Rather, meaning is understood in terms of an interaction between the reader and the text.⁴ In other words, meaning is not something to be reconstructed, but, rather, is something the reader discovers through an act of dialogue with the text. Jeffrey Boss captures the essence of such a hermeneutic when he writes, "If one reads not simply about Job, but also sees oneself as traveling Job's journey with him, then it is possible for the reader to be changed or enriched by the experience."⁵ As with other contextual hermeneutics, a logotherapy hermeneutic will be conscious of its specific bias, its specific location in place and time. This location is defined by Frankl's logotherapy and existential analysis. Boss continues, "As the story of Job unfolds it has theological and philosophical implications, and these in turn raise psychological questions."⁶ The hermeneutic will be one in which Frankl's system of psychology—a system that specifically addresses meaning in life despite unavoidable suffering—is set in dialogue with a text that describes unavoidable suffering.

As a Holocaust survivor, Frankl had a personal stake in the effectiveness of his approach. He lived the suffering about which he wrote. Because of this, reading the Book of Job with a hermeneutic based on his understanding will provide fresh insight into meaningful responses to unjust suffering. The text when read with a logotherapy hermeneutic will present opportunities for the reader to discover her own unique meanings as she clarifies her attitudes toward pain, guilt, and death as reflected in each section of Job. The reader informed by logotherapy will actively participate with the text. As meaning is discovered through this participation, we will see that Job's final response can become a site for the transcending of suffering.

The association of hermeneutics with a system of psychology is not new. For example, Sigmund Freud's psychoanalysis is viewed as a form of hermeneutics by Paul Ricoeur.⁷ As part of Ricoeur's larger project to mediate among various theories of interpretation, he argues that objective models, such as psychoanalysis, are not incompatible with hermeneutics when

---

3. Klemm, *Hermeneutical Inquiry*, vol. 1, 37.
4. Klemm, *Hermeneutical Inquiry*, vol. 1, 37.
5. Boss, *Human Consciousness of God*, Preface.
6. Boss, *Human Consciousness of God*, Preface.
7. Ricoeur, *Freud and Philosophy*, 8.

hermeneutics is conceived of as either practical philosophy or ontology.[8] Ricoeur views hermeneutics as developing in two directions. One direction is "archaic" and belongs "to the infancy of mankind." Psychoanalysis exemplifies this direction inasmuch as Freud reduces the meanings of dreams, symbols, and religion to primitive psychodynamic processes. The other direction is said to "anticipate our spiritual adventure." It is understood as a "recollection of meaning."[9] Consequently, logotherapist and psychoanalyst Stephen Costello situates Frankl within Ricoeur's meaning-oriented hermeneutic.[10] Such a hermeneutic renounces psychoanalytic reductionism as does Frankl.[11]

Ricoeur has called another psychological model for understanding the Book of Job, Carl Jung's *Answer to Job*, "one of the most important spiritual texts of the twentieth century."[12] What might be described as Jung's hermeneutic discerns within the text of Job the beginning of a transformation in the very nature of God, or, at least, in the image of God in the Western psyche.[13] This transformation includes the incorporation of the divine feminine within the Godhead through the introduction of the wisdom poem (Sophia/Logos) in chapter 28, a growth in consciousness and in the capacity to love, and an integration of the dark and light sides of God through a reconsideration of the problem of evil.[14] However, whereas Jung emphasizes changes in the consciousness of God, a logotherapy hermeneutic will explore changes in the consciousness of the reader of Job.[15]

Historically, various terms have been used to describe Frankl's concepts. Frankl coined the term *"Existenzanalyse"* in 1938 as an alternative to the earlier term "logotherapy."[16] *Existenzanalyse* was translated into English as "existential analysis." Ludwig Binswanger coined the term *"Daseinsanalyse"* in 1942 to describe his system of analysis that is closely associated with

8. Klemm, *Hermeneutical Inquiry*, vol. 1, 228.
9. Ricoeur, *Freud and Philosophy*, 496, 28.
10. Costello, *Hermeneutics*, 15.
11. Ricoeur, *Freud and Philosophy*, 27; Costello, *Hermeneutics*, 10–11; Frankl, *Man's Search for Ultimate Meaning*, 28.
12. Spiegelman, "Jung's Answer to Job," 1.
13. Jung, "Answer to Job," 3–4.
14. Spiegelman, "Jung's Answer to Job," 7–11.
15. Jung states, "Job is no more than the outward occasion for an inward process of dialectic in God." Jung, "Answer to Job," 16.
16. Frankl, "Zur geistigen Problematik der Psychotherapie," 33; Frankl, "Philosophie und Psychotherapie," 707.

Martin Heidegger's philosophy. This term also came to be translated as "existential analysis."[17] Frankl, who enjoyed an amicable relationship with Binswanger, wished to refrain from using the term "existential analysis" in his English publications to avoid confusion.[18] Frankl explained the difference between *Existenzanalyse* and *Daseinsanalyse* in 1958 and noted that the two terms were translated similarly in English, Spanish, and French. *Daseinsanalyse* according to Frankl deals with the illumination of being, while *Existenzanalyse* deals with the illumination of meaning.[19]

Following Frankl's death in 1997, the Viktor Frankl Institute of Logotherapy in the United States began to write of "Franklian Psychology" and retitled their curriculum with this term. However, the phrase was not adopted widely outside the coursework of the Institute.[20] More recently, the Viktor Frankl Institute in Vienna, Austria has advocated use of the phrase "logotherapy and existential analysis" based on the subtitle of Frankl's first book dedicated to the topic, *Arztliche Seelsorge: Grundlagen der Logotherapie und Existenzanalyse*. This phrase appears in the subtitle of Alexander Batthyány's recent volume *Existential Psychotherapy of Meaning: Handbook of Logotherapy and Existential Analysis*. Moreover, Batthyány states flatly in his Introduction to *The Feeling of Meaninglessness: A Challenge to Psychotherapy and Philosophy*: "Frankl gradually developed Logotherapy into the independent psychotherapy system that is known today as *Logotherapy and Existential Analysis*."[21] The Institute in Vienna considers the era of various "schools" of psychology to be over, rendering the adjective "Franklian" obsolete.[22]

I will use the term "logotherapy hermeneutic," and sometimes simply "logotherapy," to refer to the reading based on Frankl's thought developed here. This is based on Frankl's stated preference that the term "logotherapy" be used when referring to his ideas in English.[23] He notes, "Often I speak

17. See Binswanger, *Grundformen und Erkenntnis menschlichen Daseins*.
18. Frankl, *Recollections*, 113; Frankl, *The Will to Meaning*, 5.
19. Frankl, *The Feeling of Meaninglessness*, 81.
20. Graber, personal communication, December 1, 2012.
21. Batthyány, "Introduction," 7; italics original.
22. Batthyány, "Open Microphone Question and Answer Period," March 18, 2012.
23. Neither translations of Frankl's German works nor Frankl's books originally published in English (*The Will to Meaning* and *Man's Search for Ultimate Meaning*) typically adhere to the current English use of inclusive language. This is due partly to the era in which the works were written and translated and due partly to the nature of Frankl's native German language. This book will conform to current English conventions for

of logotherapy even in a context where no therapy in the strict sense of the word is involved."[24] At the same time, it is noted that Frankl sometimes defines logotherapy strictly in the clinical sense, defining it as "the clinical application of our existential analytic approach."[25] Based on this more restricted definition, a logotherapy hermeneutic may also be described as a "special existential analysis," or the analysis of meaning of a specific person (or text, in this case).[26]

STATEMENT OF THE PROBLEM

The central problem in the Book of Job, according to the text itself, is the issue of disinterested piety. As the satan queries in 1:9, "Does Job serve God for nothing?"[27] Moshe Greenberg explains the problem this way: "A pious man whose life has always been placid can never know whether his faith in God is an interested bargain . . . only when misfortune erupts into a man's life can he come to know the basis of his relation to God."[28] He continues, "By demonstrating that disinterested devotion to God can indeed exist is

---

inclusive language, but no attempt will be made to modify Frankl's English writings or to modify the translations of Frankl published by others. At the time of this writing, the Viktor Frankl Institute Vienna and the Viktor Frankl Archives have catalogued Frankl's publications. Some writings still remain unpublished. A German language collection of the complete works of Viktor Frankl is currently being published. The English translation of the collected works that appears subsequently is likely to address issues of inclusive language. At present, however, only the first generation translations are available.

24. Frankl, *The Will to Meaning*, 5. Unlike books published prior to 1969, *The Will to Meaning* was first published in English rather than German and has been called Frankl's "American book." Perhaps this is the occasion for Frankl's greater reflection on English terminology at this time.

25. Frankl, *Man's Search for Ultimate Meaning*, 67.

26. Frankl, *The Doctor and the Soul*, 176. The special existential analysis of a given individual (or text, in this case) is in contrast to the general existential analysis that encompasses Frankl's thoughts on such matters as the meaning of life, the meaning of death, the meaning of love, and so forth.

27. All translations are the responsibility of the author unless otherwise indicated and based on the Masoretic text. Translations are made as literally as possible except when to do so obscures the meaning. Brackets set off English words added for clarity that have no correspondence in the Hebrew. Throughout, "the satan" is used for השׂטן with the definite article and in lower case letters to indicate that the word is used as a description of function (accuser/adversary) and not as the ontological source of evil that develops in later tradition.

28. Greenberg, *The Book of Job*, xviii.

necessary for a man's spiritual well being... The terrible paradox is that no righteous man can measure his love of God unless he suffers a fate befitting the wicked."[29] John H. Eaton similarly restates the book's central question: "Do men love good, or love God, *purely*, for the sake of what they love? Or does self-interest turn even their best loves into a form of self-seeking?"[30]

Closely intertwined with this problem is the formation of a meaningful human response to unjust suffering. Norman C. Habel defines the problem this way: "The crisis of Job is not only the problem of unjustified suffering but also the question of the meaning of life when there is no future, no justice, no relief, and no purpose that he can discern."[31] In Job, the nature of God is also called into question. As Habel points out, "The way in which God agrees to test Job's integrity... raises serious doubts about God's own integrity."[32] The focus of the book, though, is on Job and not God. Job, the righteous, is confronted with a world in which righteousness is not rewarded or acknowledged. Job and his friends explore the justice of his suffering. Academic debate and orthodox belief is set against real world pain and suffering.

Job is thus confronted with the question of continuing his own existence: Will he curse God and die? At first, Job's response seems as pious as it does unambiguous: "Yahweh has given and Yahweh has seized; the Name of Yahweh be blessed" (1:21). Job's second response appears a bit more qualified. In 2:10b we read, "In all this, Job did not sin with his lips." Did he sin in his mind? Carol A. Newsom does not think so, but notes that subtle differences between Job's first and second responses have drawn attention since antiquity. In the first response, Job blesses God; in the second he does not.[33] Job's final response in 42:5–6 following the divine speeches remains ambiguous.

According to Habel, historically the ambiguity has been addressed in one of four ways.[34] Some see Job's response as complete surrender. John E. Hartley, for example, states, "A person can triumph over suffering through faith in God."[35] He does take seriously the issue of disinterested

29. Greenberg, *The Book of Job*, xviii.
30. Eaton, *Job*, 41–42.
31. Habel, *The Book of Job*, 63.
32. Habel, *The Book of Job*, 61.
33. Newsom, *The Book of Job*, 61.
34. Habel, *The Book of Job*, 577.
35. Hartley, *The Book of Job*, 50.

piety reflected in the satan's question, "Does Job fear God for nothing?" However, he argues that Job abandons his vow of innocence as an act of submission to God that leads to his vindication and restoration.[36] Others see reconciliation through Job's increased understanding of God. This is the theme of Boss, who sees Job enacting a drama that changes his consciousness of God, finally, perhaps, transcending theology.[37] He views Job's final statement as a turning away from a previous understanding toward a new sense of meaning.[38] Others view Job's response as ironic or as exposing the blindness of God. Dermot Cox, for example, places Job within the literature of the absurd.[39] He does not view Job as gaining a new sense of meaning; rather, he views Job as accepting the absurdity of the world as it has always been.[40] Others see Job's response as an act of defiance. Walter L. Michel writes that Job "passes the ultimate test" by rejecting a God described as "pompous and abusive."[41] He supports this position by arguing for the existence of ellipses in 42:5–6 that allow for a reading wherein Job comes to despise and pity God.[42] Somewhat novelly, Newsom writes of a "Bakhtinian loophole" left in its various understandings and notes that Job's response reserves "the possibility of a word yet to be spoken."[43]

The logotherapy hermeneutic and reading of the Book of Job offered below shares with many of these works important critical perspectives. The work of Cox, *The Triumph of Impotence: Job and the Tradition of the Absurd*, is an existential discussion on the meaning of Job that places the book within the tradition of the literature of the absurd, along with Samuel Beckett, Albert Camus, and Eugene Ionesco. Cox bases his argument on the proposition that Job was written at a time when the human person came to be viewed as an individual rather than as part of a collective. This then raises the issue of individual justice—and its apparent failure—that the Book of Job explores. It is the contradiction between belief in justice and the reality of human suffering that gives rise to the notion of the absurd. Cox notes that the cultural disintegration of the Austro-Hungarian Empire produced

---

36. Hartley, *The Book of Job*, 50.
37. Boss, *Human Consciousness of God*, Preface.
38. Boss, *Human Consciousness of God*, 214.
39. Cox, *The Triumph of Impotence*, 23.
40. Cox, *The Triumph of Impotence*, 156.
41. Michel, "Did Job or God Repent?," 1, 6.
42. Michel, "Did Job or God Repent?," 6.
43. Newsom, *The Book of Job*, 234.

Franz Kafka (who is one generation removed from Frankl); a similar disintegration of ancient Israel, Cox asserts, produced both Job and Qoheleth. Cox argues that cultural disintegration in both cases produced a "sense of dispossession" characterized by loss of tradition, loss of understanding, and loss of meaning. Cox states, "All explanations of ultimate meaning have been seen to be illusions."[44]

The God speeches and Job's response to them form the literary heart of the Book of Job as seen by Cox; other elements, such as the dialogue with the friends, are seen as mere foils. Cox explains, "There are no answers—but in what Job has learned we do at least come to understand what the human situation is. What *has* he learned? He has recognized the fact of absurdity, he has seen God but learned nothing new about him—except that he is in control, and that his control and his plan are beyond human comprehension."[45] Somewhat surprisingly given his understanding of the absurd, Cox argues that the God speeches reveal that an unknowable purpose, an ultimate meaning, does exist. Cox explains, "the solution offered to Job is not a future hope, but the chance of grasping a present reality; not of understanding it, but of opening a door in the cage of the absurd." He continues, "Thus, instead of locking oneself up in the prison of total non-involvement, man must keep going down the road; still in pain, still not understanding, but knowing that there is somewhere a meaning and reaching out to it."[46] Job is restored to his life by acceptance of the mystery of the ultimate and by taking responsibility for his own being. In other words, he actualizes the potentials of the situation through the discovery of his own impotence. Although a logotherapy reading, also, makes use of an existential perspective, the conclusions drawn through a logotherapy lens are much less pessimistic.

Newsom focuses her attention on reading Job as a text of many voices. Her project is to restore genre as a critical category for understanding the Book of Job, but to do so with a more robust theory than has previously been attempted. She explains, "The composition of Job in my hypothetical scenario creates a more complex relationship between author and text on the one hand and reader and text on the other, since the 'voices' that populate the text are not just character voices but generic voices as well."[47]

44. Cox, *The Triumph of Impotence*, 24.
45. Cox, *The Triumph of Impotence*, 159; italics original.
46. Cox, *The Triumph of Impotence*, 162.
47. Newsom, *The Book of Job*, 18.

She proposes that the Book of Job is largely the work of a single author who wrote by deliberately juxtaposing genres and stylized voices that embody differing perspectives on the world.[48] For example, the prose narrative corresponds to the simple moral position of Job who accepts both good and evil from God. The dialogue with the friends reflects the complexity of human dialogue with each other and with our traditions. The wisdom poem in chapter 28 responds in a sense to these genres by declaring wisdom to be inaccessible.[49]

She explains her differences with past approaches by stating, "Historical-critical scholarship honed the ability to hear distinctive styles and genres. Unfortunately, ... these insights were marshaled largely in the service of arguments over authorship and composition."[50] Newsom offers a corrective by basing her reading on Mikhail Bakhtin's concept of the polyphonic text. What she means by this is that different voices within the text are read in dialogue with one another and with the reader. Consequently, she sees each of the multiple voices in the text retaining its own unique perspective with no single voice rising to a controlling position.[51] Like Newsom, a logotherapy hermeneutic views Job as a book of our own age, a text of multiple voices read in a world of multiple voices, a text in which the reader is actively involved.

An actively involved reader is one who approaches the text with the understanding that the text will challenge the reader's beliefs. The reader will find voices with which she may share an affinity and other voices with which she may not. No single voice will dominate the discussion. Newsom explains, "In the postmodern, multicultural world, one cannot escape the reality of the multiplicity of differently situated consciousnesses that continually engage one another over questions of meaning and value." She continues, "There is no culture, no tradition, no society—indeed, no person—that is not itself composed of multiple voices."[52] This same dialogue regarding meaning (Frankl calls it the "will to meaning") also forms the dialogue of a logotherapy hermeneutic.

---

48. Newsom, *The Book of Job*, 16.

49. Newsom, *The Book of Job*, 18–19.

50. Newsom, *The Book of Job*, 10.

51. Bakhtin, *Problems of Dostoevsky's Poetics*, 3, 6–8; Bakhtin, *The Dialogic Imagination*, 430–31.

52. Newsom, *The Book of Job*, 261.

Boss is the most recent author to address meaning in the Book of Job. He views the book primarily as drama, though notes that it may be viewed as other genres as well. While not unaware of multiple aspects to the Book of Job, Boss tends to emphasize reading the text as a coherent whole somewhat more than Newsom. He believes that the drama follows a path along which the conscious understanding of God changes with character development. He notes Job's "persistence in seeking meaning for his suffering" as the driving force behind this character development.[53] As with Newsom, this "will to meaning" is also the driving force behind a logotherapy hermeneutic.

As the story unfolds, Boss sees two focal points set in tension: God and Job. Job experiences God consecutively as nurturer, destroyer, self-concealing, and holy. Psychological and theological insights are gained as the reader becomes involved with the drama and with Job's changing conceptions of God.[54] Along the journey, Job discovers himself and transcends his prior beliefs. This transcendence, perhaps, borders on mystical experience. Boss explains the lack of dialogue in the epilogue by stating, "This could mean that *Job does not now encounter an aspect of God, but is with the God behind and beyond all aspects of God. This is the eternal ultimate reality.*"[55] The central insight gained, according to Boss, is "a religion which points outside itself towards what we may, unforeseen, become makes human growth possible."[56] That is to say, a religion that emphasizes human potential, even if that potential is undefined or unknown, is what makes human growth possible. A reader informed by logotherapy will also become involved with the drama and gain psychological insights, though will make use of Frankl's system of psychology to do so.

VIKTOR FRANKL'S LOGOTHERAPY

Frankl began to develop logotherapy as a young medical student and first used the term in a 1926 address to the Academic Society for Medical Psychology. He was an active member of Alfred Adler's Society for Individual Psychology until Adler expelled him from the Society due to

---

53. Boss, *Human Consciousness of God*, Preface, 8.

54. Boss, *Human Consciousness of God*, 8. Boss also makes reference to Jung's argument that God is changed by the encounter with Job.

55. Boss, *Human Consciousness of God*, 231; italics original.

56. Boss, *Human Consciousness of God*, 257.

his "unorthodox views."[57] These views included the notion that individual psychology must free itself from psychologism, or the notion that the psychiatrist could understand the symptoms of the patient by reducing them to elements of a psychiatric theory. Frankl viewed symptoms of neurosis not only as "means to an end" (the viewpoint of Adler), but also as unique means of expression. By this, Frankl means to emphasize the humanity of the patient. Neurotic symptoms are not instrumental—as is, say, the behavior of a mouse pushing a lever for a reward—but, rather, derive from the same uniquely human sphere that is also the source of art, love, and apprehension of meaning.[58]

Frankl's first manuscript on logotherapy, *Arztliche Seelsorge: Grundlagen der Logotherapie und Existenzanalyse*, was taken from his coat lining at the time of his deportation to the Theresienstadt concentration camp on 24 September 1942. Frankl lost not only his manuscript, but also his parents and his young bride of nine months to the death camps. They had been expecting a child. Frankl himself nearly died of typhus.[59] During his internment in four concentration camps, writings of fellow prisoners tell of a Frankl that spoke of unconditional meaning in life and desired to help others. Frankl returned to the development of logotherapy and existential analysis, including the rewriting of his lost manuscript, after his liberation from Turkheim on 27 April 1945.[60]

Logotherapy and Viennese Psychiatry

Logotherapy has been called the "Third School of Viennese Psychiatry" after Freud's psychoanalysis and Adler's individual psychology.[61] The description is apt since Frankl, for instance, restates Freud's motivational principle, the "pleasure principle," as the "will to pleasure" and he refers to Adler's "superiority goal" as the "will to power."[62] He contrasts his own

---

57. Batthyány, "Introduction," 7, 12.
58. Frankl, *Recollections*, 63, 60.
59. Frankl, *Recollections*, 91, 88–89, 95.
60. Batthyány, "Introduction," 26–28. For additional information on the specifics of Frankl's movements while a prisoner, see Redsand, *Viktor Frankl*, 61–81.
61. Soucek, "Die Existenzanalyse Frankls," 594.
62. For Freud's definition of the pleasure principle, see Freud, *An Outline of Psycho-Analysis*, 3, 55. For Adler's definition of the superiority goal, see Adler, *The Practice and Theory of Individual Psychology*, 13–14.

"will to meaning" with each of these motivational constructs; in fact, he sees the will to pleasure and the will to power as derivatives of the will to meaning that confuse the means of pleasure or power with the ends of finding and fulfilling meaning and purpose. Only if the will to meaning becomes frustrated does the human person become content with either of these derivatives.[63] He sees the will to pleasure as characteristic of the infant and young child, the will to power as characteristic of the adolescent, and the will to meaning as characteristic of the mature adult.[64] He also criticizes each school for attempting to reduce the meaningfulness of human experience to these baser constructs. Frankl writes: "No one will be able to make us believe that man is a sublimated animal once we can show that within him there is a repressed angel."[65]

Frankl began a correspondence with Freud when Frankl was still a high school student. He met Freud by chance as a university student. When he introduced himself, Freud reportedly knew Frankl's mailing address by heart. Sadly, the correspondence written by Freud to Frankl was confiscated by the Gestapo when Frankl was deported to Theresienstadt. Also confiscated were some case histories hand written by Freud that Frankl had in his possession.[66] Freud had been so impressed with the young Frankl that he published a paper Frankl had shared with him in the *International Journal of Psychoanalysis*.[67] Frankl was always very gracious in his remarks concerning Freud despite his dispute with aspects of psychoanalysis, and he held that his own work was an addition to the foundation that Freud had laid.[68] Frankl's respect for Freud can be seen when he writes, "And so Freud's contribution to the foundation of psychotherapy abides, and his achievement is thereby incomparable . . . no one will ever be able to measure up to him."[69]

Frankl spent two years associated with Adler's Society of Individual Psychology, from the time of his first publication in the *Journal of*

---

63. Frankl, *The Will to Meaning*, 34–35.

64. Frankl, *The Will to Meaning*, 41. Thus, the schools of Viennese psychiatry replicate human development as each builds upon the work that preceded it.

65. Frankl, *Man's Search for Ultimate Meaning*, 65.

66. Frankl, *Recollections*, 48–51.

67. Frankl, "Zur mimischen Bejahung und Verneinung," 437–38.

68. Frankl, *Man's Search for Meaning*, 25.

69. Frankl, *On the Theory and Therapy*, 239.

Individual Psychology to the time Adler expelled him from the Society in 1927.[70] Frankl felt that individual psychology had fallen prey to the reductionist tendencies of psychologism, but also felt that the discipline could be reformed from the inside. Consequently, he did not earlier leave the Society when two of his like-minded colleagues did so.[71] Frankl reports that Adler never spoke to him again after Frankl failed to publicly defend him when they left. He was expelled a few months later.[72] Frankl responds to the criticism that logotherapy is not substantively different from individual psychology by stating: "Who is best qualified to decide that logotherapy is still individual psychology, or that it is not—who more than Adler himself? It was he who insisted that I be expelled from the society."[73]

Frankl's Answer to Jung

Binswanger, Frankl's friend and the founder of *Daseinsanalyse*, worked under Jung at one point, but there is no record that Frankl and Jung ever met. This is surprising when one considers the similarities between them.[74] Both men worked to extend psychoanalysis through the inclusion of the spiritual aspects of the human person, Frankl through an inner spiritual unconscious and Jung through a deeper collective unconscious.[75] Both men included a concept of transcendence in their work.[76] Given Frankl's contention that logotherapy could be combined with many other forms of therapy, it seems curious that more work comparing logotherapy with Jungian approaches is not more common.[77]

Frankl credits Jung for discovering religious elements within the unconscious, but criticizes him for considering them to be instinctual and impersonal, that is, archetypical and collective. (Archetypes for Jung are

70. Frankl, "Psychotherapie und Weltanschauung," 250–52.
71. Frankl, *Recollections*, 60–63. These colleagues were Rudolf Allers and Oswald Schwarz.
72. Frankl, *Recollections*, 60–63.
73. Frankl, *Recollections*, 64.
74. Frankl, *Recollections*, 113; Spiegelman, "Jung's Answer to Job," 196.
75. Frankl, *Man's Search for Ultimate Meaning*, 31; Jung, "The Structure of the Psyche," 321.
76. Frankl, *Man's Search for Ultimate Meaning*, 59; Jung, "Conscious, Unconscious, and Individuation," 524.
77. Frankl, *On the Theory and Therapy*, 185; Frankl, *Man's Search for Ultimate Meaning*, 47.

unconscious mythological themes or primordial images shared by all human beings).[78] Frankl calls this Jung's "great mistake."[79] For Frankl, unconscious religious elements belong to an existential and personal area. This means that the spiritual unconscious is not part of the mind-body organism. It operates through decisions rather than drives; it is intensely personal rather than universal. Indeed, Frankl refers to religious belief as the most personal decision that a human being makes. While religious forms are transmitted to future generations through culture, according to Frankl, each individual must embrace these forms and fill them with her own existential meaning.[80]

In explaining his differences with Jung, Frankl recounts the following exchange: "Once I was asked after one of my lectures whether I did not admit that there were such things as religious archetypes, since it was remarkable that all primitive peoples ultimately reached an identical concept of God, and this could after all only be explained with the help of a God-archetype." Frankl responded, "I asked my questioner whether there were such a thing as a Four-archetype. He did not understand immediately, and so I said, 'Look here, all people discover independently that two and two make four—we do not need an archetype for an explanation—perhaps two and two really do make four. And perhaps we do not need a divine archetype to explain human religion either—perhaps God really does exist.'"[81]

Logotherapy and American Psychology

In the United States, logotherapy is situated within Third Force psychology, an umbrella term describing a variety of humanistic and existential approaches. The central feature of these approaches compared to psychoanalysis (First Force) and behaviorism (Second Force) is an emphasis on the application of specific philosophical principles to clinical work.[82] While all such schools tend to emphasize the therapeutic relationship over testable procedures, logotherapy is distinguished from its peers by the development

---

78. Jung, "The Archetypes," 5; Storr, *The Essential Jung*, 16.
79. Frankl, *Man's Search for Ultimate Meaning*, 70.
80. Frankl, *Man's Search for Ultimate Meaning*, 70–72.
81. Frankl, *The Feeling of Meaninglessness*, 219.
82. Garfield, *Psychotherapy*, 28. The term transpersonal psychology is sometimes used to describe a Fourth Force.

of defined clinical techniques.[83] The Viktor Frankl Institute of Logotherapy, moreover, places logotherapy between the humanist-existential schools (e.g., the work of Carl Rogers, Abraham Maslow, Rollo May, Irvin Yalom, and others) and the transpersonal schools (e.g., the work of Abraham Maslow, Stanislav Grof, Michael Washburn, Fritjof Capra, and others) owing to Frankl's emphasis on self-transcendence.[84]

Frankl does not specifically disagree with behaviorism, in much the same way that he does not specifically disagree with psychoanalysis. Rather, he sees behaviorism as a discipline belonging to a lower dimension of research; logotherapy surpasses it without contradicting it. He explains this position by using the analogy of an airplane: the fact that an airplane is capable of flight does not contradict its ability to move on the ground like an automobile.[85] Frankl's interest, however, is in the specifically human capacity of noetic flight: "How should a psychotherapy that derives its conception of human nature from experiments with rats deal with the fundamental anthropological fact that persons, on the one hand, in the midst of an affluent society commit suicide, and, on the other hand, are prepared to suffer as long as that suffering has meaning?"[86]

Whereas Frankl sees logotherapy as complementary to psychoanalysis and behaviorism, he does take issue with the notion of self-actualization—a central concept in the practice of American humanist psychology. Self-actualization refers to the desire of the human person to realize individual potentials.[87] Frankl sees a concern for self-actualization as evidence of the frustration of the will to meaning and as a contradiction of the quality of self-transcendence. Like happiness, he sees self-actualization as something that cannot be pursued directly, but as something that ensues as a result of self-transcendence.[88] For Frankl, the true actualization of the self comes about only in the context of reaching beyond the self, in serving a cause solely for the sake of the cause, or in loving another solely for the sake of

---

83. Corey, *Theory and Practice*, 177.

84. Barnes, *Meaning-Centered Interventions*, 17–18.

85. Frankl, *The Will to Meaning*, 26.

86. Frankl, *On the Theory and Therapy*, 12.

87. For Maslow's definition of self-actualization, see Maslow, *Toward a Psychology of Being*, 25.

88. Frankl, *The Will to Meaning*, 38, 41.

the other. Self-actualization reduces such causes or persons to mere means for its own ends.[89]

In contrast to these traditional approaches, American psychology has seen an increasing interest in positive traits and psychological strengths in recent years.[90] The positive psychology movement reflects a shift of emphasis away from pathology and toward resilience. While this movement is not founded on logotherapy, the two approaches do share such a similar orientation that logotherapy has been described as "anticipatory" of the new movement.[91] These similarities include an acceptance of human spirituality, an emphasis on human strengths and values, an appreciation of beauty, gratitude, and humor, and an interest in a fulfilling and meaningful life.[92]

Logotherapy Today

Frankl published 32 books in his lifetime.[93] His most comprehensive treatment of logotherapy is found in *Arztliche Seelsorge: Grundlagen der Logotherapie und Existenzanalyse* published in German in 1946 and translated into English as *The Doctor and the Soul: From Psychotherapy to Logotherapy* in 1955. His final expanded thoughts appear in *Man's Search for Ultimate Meaning*, published in 1997 shortly before his death. Four texts in particular, *The Doctor and the Soul* (1955), *On the Theory and Therapy of Mental Disorders* (1956), *Man's Search for Meaning* (1959), and *The Will to Meaning* (1969) are considered foundational texts for the training of logotherapists by the Viktor Frankl Institute of Logotherapy, the organization charged with maintaining and continuing Frankl's legacy. Frankl's entire body of work is considered authoritative in defining logotherapy.

Logotherapy has been expanded by the students of Frankl. Chief among them are Joseph B. Fabry (*The Pursuit of Meaning*, 1968), Joseph B. Fabry, Reuven P. Bulka, and William S. Sahakian (*Logotherapy in Action*, 1979), Elisabeth Lukas (*Logotherapy Textbook*, 2000), Ann V. Graber

---

89. Frankl, *The Feeling of Meaninglessness*, 94.
90. Steger, et. al., "The Meaning in Life Questionnaire," 80.
91. Klingberg, "Logotherapy, Frankl, and Positive Psychology," 197.
92. Klingberg, "Logotherapy, Frankl, and Positive Psychology," 208–12.
93. Batthyány, "Introduction," 31. According to Hallowell, Frankl's archive contains "at least 100,000 documents" consisting of notes and manuscripts and "much of that work remains unpublished." Hallowell, "LogoTalk Episode 22." Two additional books were published in German in 2005 and one in English in 2010.

(*Viktor Frankl's Logotherapy*, 2004), Alexander Batthyány and Jay Levinson (*The Existential Psychotherapy of Meaning: Handbook of Logotherapy and Existential Analysis*, 2009), and Alexander Batthyány (*Logotherapy and Existential Analysis: Proceedings of the Viktor Frankl Institute Vienna, Volume 1*, 2016). Logotherapy was introduced into the Russian Federation by Snezhana Zamalieva (*Man Decides for Himself: Viktor Frankl's Logotherapy and Existential Anthropology*, 2012), the first Russian author to summarize Frankl's life and thought. A logotherapy curriculum has been developed largely by Elisabeth Lukas in Germany and by Robert C. Barnes, George E. Rice, and Paul Welter in the United States. Fourteen peer-review journals devoted to logotherapy are published around the world.[94]

Of special importance to the development of a logotherapy hermeneutic, the interpretation of film and literature has become something of a tradition within the discipline.[95] This tradition began, perhaps, because Frankl himself wrote a dramatic play days after his liberation from the concentration camps. *Synchronization in Buchenwald* has been adopted as a text by the Viktor Frankl Institute of Logotherapy in the United States and is used in the training of logotherapists. The play is performed regularly in the Russian Federation by logotherapy students at the Moscow Institute of Psychoanalysis. Although Frankl makes no mention of Job in the play, Fabry nevertheless writes of it, "In this drama . . . sufferers in a concentration camp . . . grapple with the eternal question first raised by Job: Why do we have to suffer? What is the meaning of an apparently meaningless situation?"[96]

Despite the affinities of Frankl's thought with the main themes of Job, it is curious that the only published work to date that has attempted to relate logotherapy to the Book of Job is a five-page article that appeared in *The International Forum for Logotherapy* in 1984. In this article, Alan J. Atlas asserts that both Job and Frankl address the issue of human suffering. The article uses the Book of Job to explain basic logotherapy ideas in the context of pastoral counseling, but does not attempt to develop or define a

---

94. The most important of these are *The International Forum for Logotherapy* published in the United States by the Viktor Frankl Institute of Logotherapy and *The International Journal of Logotherapy and Existential Analysis* (formerly *Journal des Viktor-Frankl-Institut*) published in Austria by the Viktor Frankl Institute Vienna.

95. This tradition continues today in the form of a standing section in *The International Forum for Logotherapy* entitled "Movies of Interest to Logotherapists."

96. Fabry, "Introduction," 1.

hermeneutic.[97] The text of Job is largely secondary to the approach and is used exclusively for purposes of illustration.

Atlas begins his article with these lines: "All people at some time in their lives are forced to suffer innocently. This undeserved agony is older than the *Book of Job* and will exist as long as humanity itself. The phenomenon of suffering and reflection on its cruelty have destroyed the faith of many, and yet preserved that of others."[98] Here, Atlas defines the scope of his argument—it is to be about human suffering and faith. His conclusion retains the same scope: "Like Job, the logotherapeutic patients are educated to realize that their problem *may not* be answered, and perhaps, *need not* be answered. Frankl and Job teach the patient and the student respectively to have unconditional trust in a very conditional life."[99]

Almost all published examples of logotherapy literary interpretation follow a pastoral counseling structure similar to that of Atlas. The longest such project to date is Robert Leslie's examination of logotherapy and the life of Christ. Leslie makes no claim that he is examining either Frankl or the ministry of Jesus from a scholarly standpoint. Rather, he develops his approach for the Christian lay reader. The focus of his work is to illustrate characteristics of personal relationships in the context of pastoral counseling.[100] Leslie describes a logotherapy principle, illustrates it with an example from a gospel narrative, and offers a pastoral opinion based on the comparison between the two, often making reference to additional psychological research and to insights gained through working with people in counseling. He states from the outset, "Our purpose here is less critical than it is therapeutic; that is, we are concerned with finding in the various incidents hints about personal relationships that are directly and immediately applicable to daily living."[101] The way in which he combines logotherapy and biblical material is described in this way: "Although the main purpose of this book is to come to a better understanding of how Jesus characteristically worked with people, the work of Frankl has been introduced in a logical order which sets forth the outline of his therapeutic approach. Thus while each chapter stands as a unit in itself and demonstrates a specific feature of the ministry of Jesus, the unfolding of Frankl's logotherapy provides

---

97. Atlas, "Logotherapy and the Book of Job," 29–33.
98. Atlas, "Logotherapy and the Book of Job," 29; italics original.
99. Atlas, "Logotherapy and the Book of Job," 33; italics original.
100. Leslie, *Jesus and Logotherapy*, 7.
101. Leslie, *Jesus and Logotherapy*, 8.

a unifying strand."[102] Leslie's goal—like that of Atlas—is to offer pastoral counseling; this they both do well.

The first attempt to bring a text into genuine dialogue with logotherapy is a 2008 article by Micah Sadigh.[103] The text is Tolstoy's *The Death of Ivan Ilyich* that Sadigh states was an influence on Heidegger as acknowledged in *Being and Time*.[104] Despite the space limitations of a journal article, Sadigh remains close to the text, following the narrative chronologically. He then amplifies certain character developments with insights from logotherapy. In contrast to the two previous examples, Sadigh's approach focuses on understanding the text through logotherapy rather than illustrating logotherapy itself.

Brief, simple examples cannot be extracted from this particular article. Rather, what Sadigh does is explain a section of text at length with no reference to Frankl. For example, "In the midst of all the pain and uncertainty, Ivan Ilyich caught himself traveling into the past. It was only in the past where he found any semblance of comfort. Finally his inner thoughts began to guide him to an insight, which resulted in a profound, inner transformation."[105] He then breaks his summary of the narrative with statements by or explanations of Frankl, "The meaning of human existence is threatened not only by suffering but also by guilt and death . . . And what about death—does it not completely cancel the meaning of our life? By no means! As the end belongs to the story, so death belongs to life."[106] Sadigh then continues his discussion of the text, "It was shortly after Ivan confessed to himself, once and for all, that he had lived an inauthentic, false life that he finally encountered a course of action . . . At the same time, the dreaded fear of death had completely left him. In a brief moment, instead of the darkness of uncertainty 'there was light.'"[107] Sadigh has since expanded his thoughts in *Existential Journey: Viktor Frankl and Leo Tolstoy on Suffering, Death, and the Search for Meaning* (2014).

---

102. Leslie, *Jesus and Logotherapy*, 9.

103. Sadigh, "Transcending Inauthenticity, Meaninglessness, and Death," 82–88.

104. Heidegger, *Being and Time*, 254, n. 12.

105. Sadigh, "Transcending Inauthenticity, Meaninglessness, and Death," 87.

106. Sadigh, "Transcending Inauthenticity, Meaninglessness, and Death," 87. The quote Sadigh uses is found in Frankl, *Psychotherapy and Existentialism*, 127–28.

107. Sadigh, "Transcending Inauthenticity, Meaninglessness, and Death," 87.

TOWARD A LOGOTHERAPY HERMENEUTIC

Logotherapy is uniquely situated to address the problem of unjust suffering and of the meaning of life in the face of it. Frankl writes, "There are situations in which one is cut off from the opportunity to do one's work or to enjoy one's life; but what never can be ruled out is the unavoidability of suffering."[108] He continues to reflect, "A bit later, I remember, it seemed to me that I would die in the near future. In this critical situation, however, my concern was different from that of most of my comrades. Their question was, 'Will we survive the camp? For, if not, all this suffering has no meaning.'" Frankl reversed the question, "Has all this suffering, this dying around us, a meaning? For, if not, then ultimately there is no meaning to survival; for a life whose meaning depends on such happenstance—as whether one escapes or not—ultimately would not be worth living at all."[109]

Frankl explains logotherapy in greater detail when he writes, "Every age has its neurosis, and needs its psychotherapy. It has been reserved for our age to incorporate the capacity of man to suffer into the scope and purpose of psychotherapy. Ours is a generation tried in suffering.... Perhaps, only by means of this experience could it find its way back to the acknowledgement of the spiritual personality of man." He continues, "The new psychotherapy and its underlying conception of man were not concocted at a conference table or at a prescription desk; they took shape in the hard school of air-raid shelters and bomb craters, in Prisoner-of-War and Concentration Camps."[110] In other words, Frankl asserts that any psychotherapy that develops after the Holocaust must take account of unjust human suffering. Likewise, a hermeneutic based on Frankl's insights must take account of unjust human suffering. For purposes of a logotherapy hermeneutic, perhaps we may add that the Book of Job has its neurosis, and needs its logotherapy.

Owing to the nature of logotherapy as a form of psychotherapy, Frankl's position emphasizes an individualistic lens in the search for personal meaning. This is somewhat different from, for example, Gustavo Gutiérrez who relates the Book of Job to the suffering of the oppressed,

---

108. Frankl, *Man's Search for Meaning*, 114.
109. Frankl, *Man's Search for Meaning*, 115.
110. Frankl, *The Feeling of Meaninglessness*, 200.

especially the poor, in Latin America. Gutiérrez views suffering from more of a social-economic-political perspective than does Frankl.[111]

However, logotherapy is clearly more than a school of psychotherapy. In 1979 Sahakian stated that logotherapy "offers one of the most adequate answers to the philosophical problems of natural evil such as the existence of human suffering. In this respect, logotherapy is a philosophy of religion in addition to being a general philosophy of life."[112] Sahakian bases his argument on logotherapy's understanding that suffering is an inevitable part of being human. Thirty years later, in 2009, Batthyány notes, "Logotherapy distinguishes itself from a number of other schools of psychotherapy by its broad applicability and interdisciplinarity."[113] He explains, "one further, and we believe defining, effect of its interdisciplinarity is that Logotherapy is applicable in settings that at least at first sight would not necessarily lend themselves to be addressed in a psychiatric or psychotherapeutic context."[114]

Frankl commonly defines "logos" as "meaning."[115] Hence, his logotherapy consists of a philosophical outlook and set of psychological principles selected and integrated as a means of discovering meaning in life. I will demonstrate that Frankl's integration of philosophical outlook and psychological principles as expressed through his logotherapy and existential analysis can also be used hermeneutically to understand meaning in texts like the Book of Job. The next two chapters will situate Frankl's thought within the worlds of psychology and hermeneutics. The remaining chapters will apply the hermeneutic to the Book of Job.

---

111. See Gutiérrez, *On Job*.
112. Sahakian, "Logotherapy's Place in Philosophy," 58–59.
113. Batthyány, *Existential Psychotherapy of Meaning*, 24.
114. Batthyány, *Existential Psychotherapy of Meaning*, 24.
115. Frankl, *The Feeling of Meaninglessness*, 61. "Meaning" is Frankl's pragmatic translation for this theologically and philosophically rich term; this bears some similarity to one of Thayer's second (mental) definitions of the term, namely, "reason, cause, ground," and to Thayer's third definition as used in the Gospel of John, in part, "the cause of all the world's life." Thayer, *The New Thayer's Greek-English Lexicon*, 381–82.

2

Viktor Frankl's Logotherapy

IN ADDITION TO BEING a system of psychotherapy, Frankl set for logotherapy the larger goal of challenging reductionism, psychologism, and nihilism. For Frankl, reductionism—the idea that a phenomenon is nothing but the sum of its parts—and the application of reductionism to psychology, which he called psychologism—the idea that human experience can be explained through nothing but psychological principles—are the contemporary expression of nihilism, or the denial of objective meaning in the world and in human experience.[1] Indeed, Frankl saw these positions as being in part responsible for the Holocaust.[2] In order to challenge these ideas, Frankl developed a number of terms and concepts. It will be helpful to provide an overview of these terms and concepts inasmuch as a logotherapy hermeneutic will use Frankl's terminology in a way consistent with his system of psychology. As will be seen, many of the positions Frankl has taken in the field of psychology run parallel to positions taken by postmodern thinkers in hermeneutics, many of whom also challenge reductionism, psychologism, and nihilism. This parallelism in thought suggests that a logotherapy hermeneutic represents an important voice in an ongoing dialogue, a voice that has not yet been heard in this context.

---

1. Frankl, *Recollections*, 59–60.
2. Frankl, *The Feeling of Meaninglessness*, 220.

THE EXISTENTIAL VACUUM

A lack of recognized meaning and purpose in life is what Frankl calls the *existential vacuum*, a state he believes is the result of the frustration of the will to meaning.[3] His definition of the idea, his description of its effect, and finally, his understanding of its ultimate resolution will provide points of reference for a logotherapy hermeneutic as it approaches the text.

Frankl describes a person experiencing the existential vacuum as living in a world in which previous traditions and values no longer provide guidance on what to do and a world in which the person may not even know what she wishes to do. A person in this situation may then simply do what others do (conformism) or do what others tell her to do (totalitarianism).[4] Manifestations of the existential vacuum include boredom, apathy, and sometimes *noogenic neurosis*, a clinical term devised by Frankl to describe psychological symptoms caused by moral and spiritual conflicts.[5]

The existential vacuum can also affect attitudes. It may be characterized by: (1) a provisional attitude toward life—living as if there is no tomorrow; (2) a fatalistic attitude toward life—acting as if one has no control over one's destiny; (3) collectivist thinking—a denial of one's own personhood; and (4) fanaticism—a denial of the personhood of those who think differently.[6] Frankl argues that these attitudes lead to the nihilism that he believes is in part responsible for the Holocaust.[7] "I am absolutely convinced," writes Frankl, "that the gas chambers of Auschwitz, Treblinka and Majdanek, were ultimately not prepared in some Ministry or other in Berlin but rather at the desks and in the lecture halls of Nihilistic scientists and philosophers."[8]

The solution to the existential vacuum, according to Frankl, is the development of a sound philosophy of life. Such a philosophy would demonstrate that life has meaning for each and every human person no matter how dire the circumstances.[9] Frankl tells of a time when he was invited to speak to prisoners on death row at the San Quentin State Prison. He

---

3. Frankl, *The Will to Meaning*, 84; Frankl, *The Feeling of Meaninglessness*, 61.
4. Frankl, *The Will to Meaning*, 83.
5. Frankl, *The Will to Meaning*, 85; Frankl, *On the Theory and Therapy*, 161–62.
6. Frankl, *On the Theory and Therapy*, 161.
7. Frankl, *The Feeling of Meaninglessness*, 216–20.
8. Frankl, *The Feeling of Meaninglessness*, 220.
9. Frankl, *The Will to Meaning*, 84.

was asked to address some of his remarks to one prisoner in particular who was to be executed in a gas chamber four days later. He writes, "How could I cope with this assignment? Resorting to personal experiences at another place where people had to face a gas chamber, I expressed my conviction that either life is meaningful—in which case its meaning does not depend upon its duration—or else it is meaningless, in which case it would be pointless to prolong it."[10] Frankl then gave an example from literature—Tolstoy's *The Death of Ivan Ilyich*—concerning the discovery of meaning even when circumstances seem meaningless.

For Frankl, once meaning is discovered, it has been brought into existence for all time. He states: "Man must make his choice concerning the mass of present potentials: which will be condemned to non-being and which one shall be actualized, and thus rescued for eternity? Decisions are final for the only really transitory aspects of life are the potentialities. When one is actualized, it is actualized forever and can never be destroyed."[11] What Frankl means is that once one discovers a meaning in a situation, then what was previously a meaning potential becomes an actual, experienced meaning. It has taken on existence through an act of human choice and thus becomes real. Frankl further explains:

> For as soon as we have used an opportunity and have actualized a potential meaning, we have done so once and for all. We have rescued it into the past wherein it has been safely delivered and deposited. In the past, nothing is irretrievably lost, but rather, on the contrary, everything is irrevocably stored and treasured. To be sure, people tend to see only the stubble fields of transitoriness but overlook and forget the full granaries of the past into which they have brought the harvest of their lives: the deeds done, the loves loved, and last but not least, the sufferings they have gone through with courage and dignity.[12]

Frankl believes that discovering and actualizing meaning in the present (or future) can even bring meaning to a meaningless past characterized by the existential vacuum. The discovery of meaning, then, represents overcoming the past and is, therefore, a human achievement. In the case of the prisoner on death row, if he chose to face his death with dignity and courage, then he made those values real in his life and, consequently, his life

---

10. Frankl, *The Will to Meaning*, 76.
11. Frankl, *The Feeling of Meaninglessness*, 100.
12. Frankl, *Man's Search for Meaning*, 150.

will forever be defined in part by them. Frankl explains that he had "hoped to show the prisoners that man can rise above himself, grow beyond himself—even in the last moment—and by so doing retroactively invest meaning even in a wasted life."[13]

Frankl gives another example of investing meaning into a wasted life in the case of Dr. J. When Frankl knew him, he was known as the "mass murderer of Steinhof." Steinhof was the primary psychiatric hospital in Vienna at the time the Nazi government began its euthanasia program. Dr. J was known for the zeal with which he worked to ensure that no person experiencing a psychosis escaped death. At the end of the war, Dr. J was captured by the Russians and eventually died in a Moscow prison. Years later, a former Austrian diplomat who was held for a time in the same prison asked Frankl if he had known Dr. J. When Frankl indicated that he had, the diplomat described Dr. J as "the best comrade you can imagine! He gave consolation to everybody. He lived up to the highest conceivable moral standard."[14] With respect to such defeat of the existential vacuum, Frankl goes on to remark, "How can we dare to predict the behavior of man?"[15]

THE CATEGORICAL VALUES

Frankl recognizes three ways in which meaning is discovered; these are known as the *categorical values* or, less frequently, the *meaning triad*. They are the creative value, the experiential value, and the attitudinal value. The *creative value* encompasses all acts that give something to life that would not otherwise exist. The creative value may be actualized through work, through hobbies, or through doing good deeds. The *experiential value* includes all experiences of truth and beauty discovered in the world as well as all loving encounters with other human beings. The experiential value may be actualized through nature, art, dance, music, literature, and through relationships of love and acceptance. To illustrate these values Frankl recalls a suicidal companion in a concentration camp who thought that there was nothing more that he could ask of life. Frankl reversed the question by asking the man if life still demanded something of him. The man replied that he had been writing a series of books that had not yet been finished and

13. Frankl, *The Will to Meaning*, 76–77.
14. Frankl, *Man's Search for Meaning*, 132.
15. Frankl, *Man's Search for Meaning*, 132.

that he had family members in another country that would be waiting for him if he survived; in other words, he replied with creative and experiential values. However, the *attitudinal value* is considered by Frankl to be superior to both the creative and experiential values. The attitudinal value is actualized through the stance taken toward unavoidable suffering. If one chooses bravery over cowardice, mercy over revenge, or justice over appeasement, then the attitudinal value has been actualized. A meaningful life is a life in which these values are actualized to the greatest possible degree.[16]

FRANKL'S ASSUMPTIONS AND THE WILL TO MEANING

Frankl makes three assumptions about the nature of being human that will necessarily influence a logotherapy hermeneutic. As stated by Frankl, these are freedom of the will, the will to meaning, and meaning in life. *Freedom of the will* refers to freedom to choose one's response to the conditions of life; it is not freedom from conditions in life.[17] Indeed, Frankl writes of the *tragic triad*, or those conditions of life from which no human being can escape: pain, guilt, and death.[18] Frankl sees a fluid boundary between the *area of freedom* and the *area of fate*. At times, the area of freedom may be large with many opportunities to actualize values. At other times, the area of freedom may be small, but it never reduces to zero. Frankl famously writes: "We who lived in concentration camps can remember the men who walked through the huts comforting others, giving away their last piece of bread. They may have been few in number, but they offer sufficient proof that everything can be taken from a man but one thing: the last of the human freedoms—to choose one's attitude in any given set of circumstances, to choose one's own way."[19]

The *will to meaning*, or the desire to understand the purpose of one's own life, is the basic human motivation in logotherapy.[20] As noted, Frankl sees it as more basic than even the desire for pleasure and the desire to avoid pain. In fact, he points out that the human person will sacrifice pleasure or choose to undergo pain if it is seen has having a transcendent mean-

---

16. Frankl, *The Will to Meaning*, 70; Frankl, *The Feeling of Meaninglessness*, 118; Frankl, *Man's Search for Meaning*, 111, 112–15, 141–42.
17. Frankl, *The Will to Meaning*, 16.
18. Frankl, *The Will to Meaning*, 73.
19. Frankl, *Man's Search for Meaning*, 65–66.
20. Frankl, *The Feeling of Meaninglessness*, 61–62.

ing for the sake of another or for a cause in which one believes.[21] Finally, meaning in life is believed to be an objective *demand characteristic* of the environment.[22] One of Frankl's most important insights is that it is not the human person who asks the meaning of life, but, rather, life that asks something of the human person. He explains: "One should not search for an abstract meaning of life. Everyone has his own specific vocation or mission in life to carry out a concrete assignment which demands fulfillment. Therein he cannot be replaced, nor can his life be repeated. Thus, everyone's task is as unique as is his specific opportunity to implement it."[23] Moreover, logotherapy teaches that life has meaning under any and all circumstances. Meaning in life is unconditional.[24] It is not the task of the human person to invent a meaning, but to discover the meaning that is already present.[25]

To illustrate the discovery of meaning, Frankl tells the story of his consideration of accepting an American visa to emigrate after the Nazis had annexed Austria:

> Shortly before the United States entered World War II I received an invitation from the American Embassy in Vienna to go there to pick up my visa for immigration to this country. At that time I was living in Vienna alone with my old parents. They, of course, did not expect me to do anything but pick up the visa and then hurry to this country. But at the last moment I began to hesitate because I asked myself, 'Should I really? Can I do it at all?' For it suddenly came to my mind what was in store for my parents. . . . Then I went home and when I did so, I noticed a piece of marble stone lying on a table. I inquired of my father how it came to be there, and he said, "Oh, Viktor, I picked it up this morning at the site where the synagogue stood." (It had been burned down by the National Socialists.) "And why did you take it with you?" I asked him. "Because it is a part of the two tables containing the Ten Commandments." And he showed me, on the marble stone, a Hebrew letter engraved and gilded. "And I can tell you even more," he continued, "if you are interested; this Hebrew letter serves as the abbreviation of only one of the Ten Commandments." Eagerly I asked him, "Which one?" And his answer was: "Honor father and mother and

---

21. Frankl, *Psychotherapy and Existentialism*, 40–41; Frankl, *Man's Search for Meaning*, 113.
22. Frankl, *Psychotherapy and Existentialism*, 21, 64.
23. Frankl, *Man's Search for Meaning*, 108–9.
24. Frankl, *Man's Search for Meaning*, 114.
25. Frankl, *Man's Search for Meaning*, 62.

you will dwell in the land." On the spot I decided to stay in the country, together with my parents, and let the visa lapse.[26]

One concrete way in which logotherapy understands the will to meaning is through the distinction it makes between *ultimate meaning* and the *meaning of the moment*. Ultimate meaning is believed to exist, but to be largely unknown or unknowable. It is the area of faith.[27] The meaning of the moment, on the other hand, is knowable. The meaning of the moment consists in the one categorical value that any given moment in life requires of any given person.[28] This must be discerned, rightly or wrongly, through the operation of conscience.[29] For Frankl, each combination of person and situation is unique and demands a unique response.[30] Nevertheless, similar meanings discovered in similar situations over time leads to the development of religions and universal values.[31] This does not excuse any given person from choosing what a unique situation may demand even if it should be in opposition to culturally accepted values.[32] He writes: "In an age in which the Ten Commandments seem to lose their unconditional validity, man must learn more than ever to listen to the ten thousand commandments arising from the ten thousand unique situations of which his life consists. And as to *these* commandments, he is referred to, and must rely on, his conscience."[33]

Frankl gives an example of realizing the meaning of the moment by noting that in one unique situation, a newly married husband was informed through conscience that he should free his wife from her marriage vows. The specific situation was that the young wife, newly arrived in a concentration camp, might be given the option to remain alive if she engaged in sexual activity with members of the SS. Frankl writes of the situation, "The unique meaning was to abandon the universal value of marital faithfulness, to disobey one of the Ten Commandments. To be sure, this was the only way to obey another of the Ten Commandments—'Thou shalt not kill.'

---

26. Frankl, *The Will to Meaning*, 58–59.
27. Frankl, *Psychotherapy and Existentialism*, 33.
28. Frankl, *Man's Search for Meaning*, 108, 110–11.
29. Frankl, *The Will to Meaning*, 57.
30. Frankl, *Man's Search for Ultimate Meaning*, 41.
31. Frankl, *The Will to Meaning*, 63.
32. Frankl, *Man's Search for Ultimate Meaning*, 42; Frankl, *The Will to Meaning*, 19, 63.
33. Frankl, *The Will to Meaning*, 65; italics original.

Not giving her his absolution would have made him co-responsible for her death."[34] Fabry informs us that this man was Frankl himself.[35]

THE NATURE OF THE HUMAN PERSON

Frankl views the human person as a spirit that has a mind and a body (a psyche and a soma). He often refers to spirit as *noos* (and uses the adjective form *noetic*) to avoid religious connotation. He states that by this term he refers to that which is "uniquely human."[36] The uniquely human realm includes such phenomena as love, freedom, and the will to meaning. The division between the spirit and the mind-body being is absolute for Frankl. The former possesses free will; the latter is subject to the laws of biology and psychology. The former is the seat of human existence; the latter is the home of somatic and psychological facticity.[37] Consequently, Frankl does not dispute objective, empirical findings, such as elements of the psychodynamic model proposed by Freud (the existence of the unconscious, for instance) or the discoveries of American behaviorism (such as classical conditioning).[38] Rather, he sees his contribution as consisting of a psychological model that includes the spirit in an understanding of the human person and in the clinical techniques derived from this model.[39] Frankl refers to this model as *dimensional ontology*.[40] He explains: "Once we have projected man into the biological and psychological dimensions we ... obtain contradictory results. Dimensional ontology is far from solving the mind-body problem. But it does explain why the mind-body problem cannot be solved. Of necessity the unity of man—a unity in spite of the multiplicity of body and mind—cannot be found in the biological or psychological but must be sought in that noological dimension out of which

---

34. Frankl, *The Will to Meaning*, 63–64.
35. Fabry, *The Pursuit of Meaning*, 62.
36. Frankl, *The Will to Meaning*, 17–18, 22. Frankl recalls an episode at the age of 13 when a teacher told the class that life was nothing but an oxidation process. The young Frankl sprang to his feet and asked, "Professor, if this is the case, what meaning then does life have?" For further discussion of Frankl's understanding of the uniquely human nature of meaning, see Frankl, *Man's Search for Ultimate Meaning*, 96. One might even argue that logotherapy is Frankl's answer to his precocious question.
37. Frankl, *Man's Search for Ultimate Meaning*, 32–33.
38. Frankl, *The Will to Meaning*, 26.
39. Frankl, *On the Theory and Therapy*, 228.
40. Frankl, *The Will to Meaning*, 23; Frankl, *The Feeling of Meaninglessness*, 63–64.

Viktor Frankl and the Book of Job

man is projected in the first place."[41] He refers to the functional aspects of the model as *noodynamics* of which he writes, "What man needs is not homeostasis but what I call 'noodynamics,' i.e., the existential dynamics in a polar field of tension where one pole is represented by a meaning that is to be fulfilled and the other pole by the man who has to fulfill it."[42]

Frankl explains his dimensional ontology graphically by use of an image of a cylinder. When the curved plane of the cylinder is viewed, it is divided into three segments representing the conscious, the preconscious, and the unconscious—terms borrowed from Freud. When viewed from either end, the cylinder is further divided into an inner spiritual core, a psyche, and an outer body (see figure 1). Frankl explains his concept of the human spirit based on this model.[43]

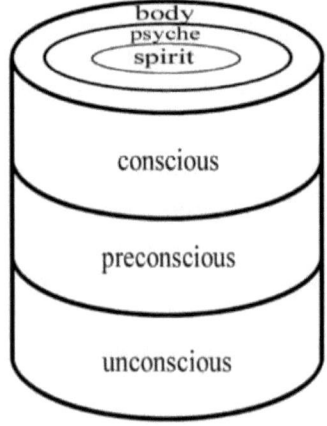

Figure 1. Frankl's Dimensional Ontology

For Frankl, evidence of the human spirit is found in those attitudes and behaviors that would not be predicted from biology and psychology. Frankl often refers to this unpredictable quality of being human as "the

---

41. Frankl, *The Will to Meaning*, 24–25.
42. Frankl, *Man's Search for Meaning*, 105.
43. Frankl, *The Will to Meaning*, 22–25; Frankl, *Man's Search for Ultimate Meaning*, 33–36 (figures 1 and 2 in this chapter are based on an unlabeled figure in Frankl, *Man's Search for Ultimate Meaning*, 35); Frankl, *The Feeling of Meaninglessness*, 75–77.

defiant power of the human spirit."[44] By this, he means the capacity of the human person to behave in accordance with meaningful values even when logic would conclude such values offer no utility. An example would be the sharing of bread between two starving people in a situation where both are likely to die regardless of whether the bread is eaten. Frankl observed this quality of being human even in a concentration camp. He notes, "There were always choices to make. Every day, every hour, offered the opportunity to make a decision, a decision which determined whether you would or would not submit to those powers which threatened to rob you of your very self, your inner freedom; which determined whether or not you would become the plaything of circumstance, renouncing freedom and dignity to become molded into the form of the typical inmate."[45]

FRANKL'S LAWS OF DIMENSIONAL ONTOLOGY

Frankl addresses the relationship between the person as a spiritual being and the empirical study of the human person through the sciences by means of his *first law of dimensional ontology*: "One and the same phenomenon projected out of its own dimension into different dimensions lower than its own is depicted in such a way that the individual pictures contradict one another."[46] Returning to the image of the cylinder, Frankl explains that, if projected from three-dimensional space onto a two dimensional plane, the cylinder may appear as either a rectangle or a circle (see figure 2). These images appear contradictory, one having height and width, the other having circumference and radius. The contradiction is only solved when one recalls that the geometry measured is only a projection of a cylinder. An error is made if one comes to believe that a cylinder is nothing but a rectangle or nothing but a circle. Likewise, an error is made if the psychologist assumes that the human person is nothing but the dynamics of the psyche or if the biologist assumes that the human person is nothing but a collection of chemicals.[47] Said another way, depression may be seen by some as a set of cognitive self-statements learned in childhood or it may be seen as a deficiency of a chemical neurotransmitter. Frankl argues that an error is made if it is seen as either of these things exclusively. Regardless of

---

44. Frankl, *Man's Search for Meaning*, 147.
45. Frankl, *Man's Search for Meaning*, 66.
46. Frankl, *The Will to Meaning*, 23.
47. Frankl, *The Will to Meaning*, 24–25.

its cause, the human spirit is able to take a defiant stance toward the depression.[48]

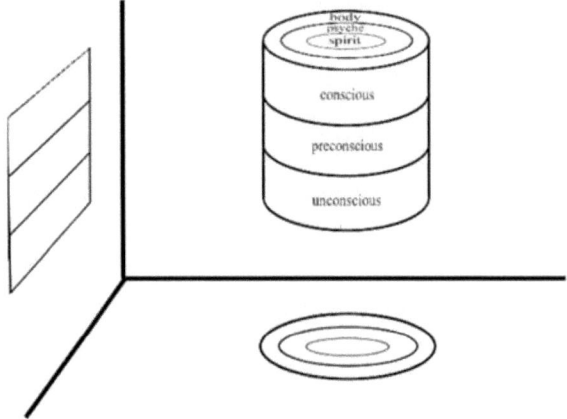

Figure 2. Frankl's First Law of Dimensional Ontology

A second analogy to explain Frankl's first law of dimensional ontology is made with the observation that the cylinder as depicted by Frankl is open, whereas the rectangular and circular projections are closed. That is, deterministic principles operate within the closed systems of psychology and biology, but freedom is found in the open system of the human spirit.[49]

Frankl's model is further explained by his *second law of dimensional ontology*: "Different phenomena projected out of their own dimension into one dimension lower than their own are depicted in such a manner that the pictures are ambiguous."[50] One may imagine that a circle may be the two dimensional projection of a cone, a cylinder, or a sphere (see figure 3). The cause of the circle is unclear. Likewise, a depression may have a physical, a psychological, or a spiritual cause.[51] Frankl sees logotherapy as the specific treatment of choice when the cause of psychological symptoms is spiritual, that is, when the cause is a conflict between what the person is and what the person may become. Because Frankl views the spiritual dimension as incorruptible, logotherapy is also seen as an ancillary treatment when a psy-

48. Frankl, *The Will to Meaning*, 123, 132–33.
49. Frankl, *The Will to Meaning*, 24–25.
50. Frankl, *The Will to Meaning*, 23.
51. Frankl, *The Will to Meaning*, 24–25.

VIKTOR FRANKL'S LOGOTHERAPY

chological disturbance has either psychological or physical causes.[52] In this latter case, the spiritual core is seen as a source of health and strength in its ability to choose an attitude toward the illness.[53]

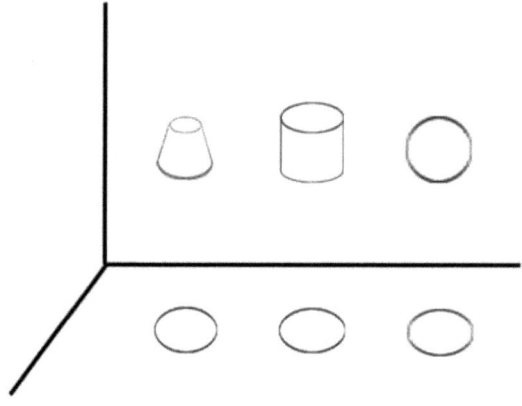

Figure 3. Frankl's Second Law of Dimensional Ontology

THE SPIRITUAL UNCONSCIOUS

As depicted by the cylinder, part of the human spirit is unconscious. The spiritual unconscious has a dynamic energy (that is, noodynamics) created by the difference between what a person is and what a person is capable of becoming.[54] To contrast his model of the unconscious with that of Freud, Frankl calls Freud's concept the *instinctual unconscious*.[55] Just as Freud associates the instinctual unconscious with libido, or unconscious sexual energy, so Frankl associates the spiritual unconscious with *religio*, or unconscious religiosity.[56] Frankl further defines this unconscious religiosity as a "latent relation to transcendence."[57] By this, Frankl means an inherent human capacity to relate to something greater than oneself. Frankl does

52. Frankl, *On the Theory and Therapy*, 185.
53. Frankl, *The Doctor and the Soul*, 289–90; Frankl, *The Feeling of Meaninglessness*, 73. (Figure 3 in this chapter is similar to Frankl's Figure 2 in *The Will to Meaning* [p. 24].)
54. Frankl, *The Feeling of Meaninglessness*, 63–64.
55. Frankl, *Man's Search for Ultimate Meaning*, 31–32.
56. Freud, *An Outline of Psycho-Analysis*, 6–7; Frankl, *Man's Search for Ultimate Meaning*, 54–55.
57. Frankl, *Man's Search for Ultimate Meaning*, 68.

not view this capacity as a drive, however, like Freud's notion of libido, but rather as a "pull" from a noetic dimension, from a place where a transpersonal awareness can perceive the potentials of the human person.[58]

Frankl expands on his notion of transcendence when he writes, "The essentially self-transcendent quality of human existence renders man *a being reaching out beyond himself*. Therefore, if Martin Buber, along with Ferdinand Ebner, interprets human existence basically in terms of a dialogue between I and Thou, we must recognize that this dialogue defeats itself unless I and Thou transcend themselves to refer to a meaning outside themselves."[59] He further explains: "If one prefers, one might conceive of this relation in terms of a relationship between the immanent self and a transcendent Thou. However one wishes to formulate it, we are confronted with what I should like to term 'the transcendent unconscious' as part and parcel of the spiritual unconscious."[60]

This *transcendent unconscious* gives rise to the conscious experience of *conscience*. Conscience, for Frankl, is essentially the tool by which meaning can be discovered. He explains, "Conscience is that capacity which empowers him [the human person] to seize the meaning of a situation in its very uniqueness, and in the final analysis meaning is something unique."[61] Frankl understands the existence of conscience to imply the existence of a transpersonal agent just as the existence of the navel implies the existence of a mother.[62] He explains, "Conscience is fully understandable only against the background of a transhuman dimension. To explain man's being free, the existential quality of human reality would do; however, to explain his being responsible, the transcendent quality of conscience must be considered."[63]

To the extent that a person chooses to respond to this pull of *religio*, the conscience becomes conscious. Unlike Freud's superego the conscience, as a function of the human spirit, remains free to take a stand for or against any given cultural norm or moral.[64] The purpose of the conscience is to

---

58. Frankl, *Man's Search for Ultimate Meaning*, 60; Frankl, *The Feeling of Meaninglessness*, 77–78.

59. Frankl, *The Will to Meaning*, 8; italics original.

60. Frankl, *Man's Search for Ultimate Meaning*, 68.

61. Frankl, *The Will to Meaning*, 19.

62. Frankl, *Man's Search for Ultimate Meaning*, 59–61.

63. Frankl, *Man's Search for Ultimate Meaning*, 61.

64. Frankl, *Man's Search for Ultimate Meaning*, 63–65. For Freud's association of the

inform the human person of the one, right thing required by any unique situation.⁶⁵ One purpose of logotherapy is to make the spiritual unconscious conscious.⁶⁶ This leads to a refinement and development of the human conscience.⁶⁷

Frankl believes that evidence of *religio* can be found through the use of tools common to psychodynamic practice such as dream interpretation and word association.⁶⁸ An example of *religio* may be found in the following dream interpretation:⁶⁹

> The dreamer works in the American health care industry. He dreams that people are forced to go into space once a year on a rocket as part of the government's attempt to reform the health care system. Rockets have been prepared for the first batch of patients. A capsule is set on top of a rocket and a parachute attached. This tall, white rocket with black accents is unusually bright against the blue sky. This procedure is too dangerous, thinks the dreamer. He and his mother are in an elevator. She is going to the rocket, but the dreamer knows it is not yet time. She tells him she is scheduled for 1:30. He is scheduled for 5:30. The vivid, white rocket is then launched. As the rocket lifts off, the billowing plumes of smoke become clouds and the white rocket becomes Christ in vivid white robes.

Whereas a Freudian interpretation of this dream might focus on the rocket as a phallic symbol and a Jungian interpretation could focus on the Christ figure as a symbol of the Self, Frankl might interpret the dream in light of *religio*. In this case, the ascent of the health care rocket latently manifests the idea of spiritual healing. As the dreamer had been reading Jung, it is likely that the mother image was chosen to represent the unconscious (with reference to what Jung calls the *anima*).⁷⁰ The fact that she is "going first" suggests that spiritual healing is taking place first in the spiritual unconscious, but that the dreamer must wait for some period of time before

---

superego with conscience, see Freud, *An Outline of Psycho-Analysis*, 62.

65. Frankl, *Man's Search for Ultimate Meaning*, 40–41.
66. Frankl, *Man's Search for Ultimate Meaning*, 43–44, 47.
67. Frankl, *The Feeling of Meaninglessness*, 183.
68. Frankl, *Man's Search for Ultimate Meaning*, 47, 69.
69. Author's private collection.
70. Jung, "Aion," 26.

becoming fully aware of it. The spiritual unconscious is preparing him for departure to spiritual health.

The transcendent aspect of the spiritual unconscious demands responsible action. Frankl states what he calls the *categorical imperative of logotherapy* as: "Live as if you were already living for the second time and had acted as wrongly the first time as you are about to act now."[71] By this Frankl challenges the human person to view conduct in a larger frame, or to consider how a given behavior may be viewed at a future point. Unlike Freud, who defines the conscience as a psychological process determined by childhood experiences (i.e., the superego), Frankl refuses to reduce the conscience to something determined by anything else. For Frankl, conscience is a matter of irreducible transcendence, a function of a free and transcendent human spirit.[72] This is an example of how Frankl rejects reductionism and psychologism and, thus, transforms psychotherapy from an applied science to an understanding of being human.

CLINICAL APPLICATIONS

While the clinical applications of logotherapy may well fall outside the scope of a literary logotherapy hermeneutic, a brief survey of them will provide a wider context in which to understand Frankl's overall project. This may be helpful in ensuring that the hermeneutic remains consistent with Frankl's overall approach.

Frankl sees the tension between what the human person is and what the human person may yet become—noodynamics—as necessary to mental health.[73] He criticizes both psychodynamic psychiatry and empirical psychology for their reliance on the principle of homeostasis—the tendency of an organism to maintain balance.[74] Frankl asserts that the role of the human spirit is not to maintain balance, but to strive toward meaning fulfillment.[75] He defines two qualities of the human spirit as freedom of the will that leads to the ability to *self-distance* and the will to meaning that

---

71. Frankl, *The Feeling of Meaninglessness*, 89.
72. Frankl, *Man's Search for Ultimate Meaning*, 63.
73. Frankl, *Man's Search for Meaning*, 103–5.
74. Frankl, *The Feeling of Meaninglessness*, 77–78.
75. Frankl, *The Feeling of Meaninglessness*, 77.

leads to the ability to *self-transcend*. Frankl's clinical methods are based on these characteristics of self-distancing and self-transcendence.[76]

Self-distancing is the ability to detach from oneself and to reflect on oneself. This allows the human person, through the exercise of the freedom of the spirit, to choose an attitude both toward the world and toward the mind-body self that is part of the world. It is through self-distancing that the human person is able to choose a response to unavoidable suffering of any kind, be it Frankl's internment in the death camps or to the mental and physical diseases that were the subject of his psychiatric practice.[77]

Frankl's clinical technique of *paradoxical intention* is based on self-distancing. The use of this technique requires that the patient wish for the very thing that elicits the greatest anxiety. (Clinically, this breaks the cycle of anxiety).[78] For example, a patient who has panic attacks may not leave home for fear that she will have a heart attack and die. Such a patient would humorously develop the attitude of trying to have as many heart attacks each day as possible, perhaps adding a stroke or two for good measure. Anticipatory anxiety in such a patient would then diminish and the patient would leave home more frequently.[79]

Self-transcendence allows the human person to discover meaning by reaching beyond herself. Frankl views this process as part of an open system, and thus spiritual, noetic, rather than as part of a closed, instinctual, biological system that he believes characterizes the existence of animals. He contrasts the capacity for self-transcendence with the homoestasis principle that he closely identifies with Freud's pleasure principle: i.e., pleasure is the fulfillment of desire and the function of the psyche is to bring desire to a rest.[80] In Frankl's view, true human existence is found in reaching beyond the self. For him, happiness cannot be pursued through pleasure, but, rather, ensues as the result of the discovery of meaning in life.[81]

Frankl's clinical technique of *dereflection* is based on the self-transcending ability.[82] Whereas paradoxical intention focuses humor on the symptom, the process of dereflection diverts attention away from the

---

76. Frankl, *The Will to Meaning*, 17–19, 99.
77. Frankl, *The Feeling of Meaninglessness*, 108–9.
78. Frankl, *The Will to Meaning*, 102.
79. Frankl, *The Will to Meaning*, 105–6.
80. Freud, *An Outline of Psycho-Analysis*, 3, 55.
81. Frankl, *The Will to Meaning*, 31–38.
82. Frankl, *The Will to Meaning*, 99.

symptom and toward a meaningful person or cause. One of many clinical examples involves a case of impotence. The patient focused his attention on whether or not he was achieving an erection, with the result that he did not. The logotherapy solution is to help the patient stop focusing on sex as technique and to begin viewing sexuality as a striving for love, that is, as a self-transcendent phenomenon. According to Frankl, such symptoms then resolve themselves.[83]

As will be seen more fully in chapter 3, Frankl used phenomenology to free himself from the preconceived psychological theories of his day. This allowed him to listen to his patients and to identify common themes that they discussed with him. Frankl's concepts derive from this clinical work and his concepts, in turn, demonstrate how he came to interpret the psychological material of his patients. As such, they provide points of reference in forming a logotherapy hermeneutic, a hermeneutic with textual application that remains true to the framework that Frankl applied clinically.

---

83. Frankl, *On the Theory and Therapy*, 127–28.

3

Logotherapy and Hermeneutics

KLEMM HELPFULLY EXPLAINS THE differences among premodern, modern, and postmodern hermeneutics. The premodern world can be said to view the text as an independent reality that communicates a specific meaning forever fixed in time. The reader understands the text through identification with it. The modern world attempts to develop tools and methods to determine the meaning of the text as an object (objectivity). Postmodern thought asserts the impossibility of objectivity and seeks understanding through dialogue between the text and the reader, who has a specific location in time and space.[1]

As we will see, a logotherapy hermeneutic is, by necessity, a postmodern hermeneutic in the sense described by Klemm if it is to remain consistent with the philosophical foundation Frankl proposed for logotherapy. The postmodern view, for example, holds that a text cannot convey an ultimate or single, stable meaning.[2] In speaking of the ultimate meaning of a human life, Frankl likewise states that the ultimate meaning cannot be known.[3] Like the postmodern interpreter, Frankl speaks of the "local" meaning of the moment.[4] Logotherapy asks, "What is the meaning of this choice at this time?" In terms of a logotherapy hermeneutic, a reader may ask, "What is the meaning of this text to this reader at this moment?"

1. Klemm, *Hermeneutical Inquiry*, vol. 1, 5–24.
2. Klemm, *Hermeneutical Inquiry*, vol. 1, 38.
3. Frankl, *Psychotherapy and Existentialism*, 33.
4. Frankl, *Man's Search for Meaning*, 108.

Klemm further explains that hermeneutics can be seen as theory of interpretation, practical philosophy, speculative ontology, or theology (or a combination of any of these). Klemm proposes a system of classifying hermeneutics depending upon whether the emphasis is on the subject (the reader), the verb (understanding), or the object (the text). He elaborates through the use of the sentence, "I understand you," where "you" in this case refers to the text (e.g., Job). In brief, an emphasis on the "you" of Klemm's sentence reflects a position that corresponds to the first, modern hermeneutics wherein meaning is discovered through conscious study of the object (the text) by means of specific tools (techniques, methods, theories). The historical-critical method is an example of this approach. Hermeneutics as practical philosophy would correspond to a focus on the verb "understand" in Klemm's sentence. Meaning is discovered through a dialogue, a specific reading of the text by a given reader at a given time. In other words, a text is understood from a certain point of view. Speculative ontology focuses on the "I" portion of Klemm's sentence. Speculative ontology deals with the meaning of being itself. These later two positions encompass the postmodern orientation. Finally, hermeneutics becomes theology when understanding is overturned by an apprehension of the divine. This overturning may take place within any of the other types.[5]

Within Klemm's system, a logotherapy hermeneutic will fall within the realm of practical philosophy. The warrant for this conclusion comes from Frankl himself. He identifies the psychotherapeutic method of choice in any given case by the following equation:

$$\Psi = x + y$$

The treatment of choice—the psychotherapeutic method or techniques recommended to the patient—represented by Ψ is the sum of the unique personalities of the patient and the therapist (x and y).[6] A logotherapy hermeneutic can likewise claim the formula:

$$L = x + y$$

Here the logotherapy hermeneutic (L) is the outcome of an interaction, or dialogue, between the reader and the text (x and y).

A logotherapy hermeneutic, then, does not seek an absolute understanding of what the text meant to the original author, nor is it free to

---

5. Klemm, *Hermeneutical Inquiry*, vol. 1, 32–53.
6. Frankl, *The Will to Meaning*, 109.

impose a meaning solely because of its position as logotherapy (hermeneutics as theory of interpretation and hermeneutics as speculative ontology, respectively).[7] Rather, a logotherapy hermeneutic will set a text in dialogue with a system of psychology that asserts that meaning is unique for every person in every situation. When applied to the Book of Job, a logotherapy hermeneutic will set a text dealing with unjust suffering in dialogue with logotherapy that asserts that meaning can be found even in a situation of unavoidable suffering.

THE COMMON ROOTS OF LOGOTHERAPY AND HERMENEUTICS

Frankl identifies logotherapy as "existential" and "phenomenological."[8] The use of these terms have converged within psychiatry and psychology where they apply to those theories that emphasize human experience over natural-scientific approaches.[9] An understanding of how this relates to hermeneutics can be gained by turning to the "common ancestors" of both logotherapy and postmodern hermeneutics: Martin Heidegger and Edmund Husserl. From here two paths emerge. One path is that of psychiatry as influenced by the contributions of Medard Boss, Ludwig Binswanger, and Max Scheler. The other path is that of hermeneutics as influenced especially by Hans-Georg Gadamer and Paul Ricoeur. Both paths move in parallel toward a position that overcomes psychologism.[10] A logotherapy hermeneutic will combine the two paths, developing a postmodern hermeneutic with the specific insights of Frankl's logotherapy.

According to Merold Westphal, the pathway of hermeneutics through Heidegger, Gadamer, and Ricoeur has no label that identifies it. He calls it "relativistic hermeneutics." What Westphal means by this is that the hermeneutics of Heidegger, Gadamer, and Ricoeur share a similar understanding of the hermeneutic circle. That is, interpretation never takes place without presumptions on the part of the reader. This is the reader's location as defined socially, culturally, historically, and linguistically. Different readers may be aware or unaware of their location to various degrees, but no reader

---

7. Klemm, *Hermeneutical Inquiry*, vol. 1, 34, 37.

8. Frankl, *The Will to Meaning*, 5–7; Frankl, *Man's Search for Ultimate Meaning*, 29; Frankl, *The Feeling of Meaninglessness*, 108.

9. Halling and Nill, "A Brief History," xxvii–xxix.

10. Frankl, *Recollections*, 59–60.

is ever located nowhere. That is, no reader is without presumptions. The reader's presumptions may change, for example, through dialogue with a text, but the reader can never eliminate the reality of having them.[11] As we have said, our hermeneutic consciously presumes the defined position of logotherapy; our reader is a logotherapist.

In addition, relativistic hermeneutics rejects psychologism. For Frankl, as we have seen, psychologism means reducing the understanding of the symptoms of a patient to nothing more than the elements of a psychiatric theory.[12] For hermeneutics other than relativistic hermeneutics, psychologism according Westphal means that the reader must come to inhabit the world, if not the mind, of the author of a text.[13] He explains the concept in the following way: "The goal of interpretation, then, is to reverse the process of writing, to work back from the expression to the inner experience."[14] He then expands by quoting Friedrich Schleiermacher, "Before the art of hermeneutics can be practiced, the interpreter must put himself both objectively and subjectively in the position of the author."[15] Analogous to Frankl's use of the term, hermeneutic psychologism reduces the text to something similar to a "symptom" produced by an author.

The rejection of psychologism, according to Westphal, allows for the rejection of objectivism, defined as the notion that "interpretation can free itself from particular perspectives and presuppositions, whether personal or communal, and give us *the* meaning of the text."[16] Moreover, *the* meaning of the text is what the author meant the text to mean, which brings us back to psychologism. He goes on to explain, "One implication of this view is that while my or 'our' current understanding of the Bible can claim to be *the* meaning of the text, the rest of Christian history is a series of unfortunate misinterpretations. Anxiety about relativism morphs into arrogance."[17] At the same time, Westphal explains that not "anything goes" in relativistic hermeneutics, but that "author and reader are cocreators of

---

11. Westphal, *Whose Community?*, 35–36.
12. Frankl, *Recollections*, 59–60.
13. Westphal, *Whose Community?*, 28–30, 36.
14. Westphal, *Whose Community?*, 30.
15. Westphal, *Whose Community?*, 30.
16. Westphal, *Whose Community?*, 46; italics original. See also Westphal, *Whose Community?*, 36.
17. Westphal, *Whose Community?*, 47; italics original.

textual meaning."[18] This accords well with Frankl's view of meaning. Although Frankl retains the word "objective" to describe meaning, by this he simply means that meaning may, in fact, be discovered; that is, it is not an "anything goes" projection of the human person.[19] Frankl states, "*Meaning is what is meant,*" but he explains that meaning remains a unique discovery of a particular person in a particular situation.[20]

Martin Heidegger

Klemm identifies Martin Heidegger as the watershed separating modern hermeneutics (attributed to Schleiermacher and Wilhelm Dilthey) from the postmodern.[21] The hermeneutic question for Heidegger is the meaning of being itself, or, rather, the manner of being for one who is capable of understanding.[22] He expresses this concept by using the German term *Dasein* in a specifically defined way that is now associated with his thought. *Da*, meaning "here" or "there," is used to signify that transcendence is intrinsic to the human person. *Sein*, or being, means that the human person is the being who questions Being and who is also open to an understanding of Being. Heidegger uses the word *Dasein* in place of the words person, conscious, or subject, but not as a mere substitute for these words. Rather, he seeks to describe a certain ontological condition characterized by questioning and understanding Being. Heidegger's *Dasein* is partly revealed and partly hidden; he suggests that hermeneutics is the means by which *Dasein* reveals itself.[23] Thus, Heidegger makes hermeneutics equivalent to ontology.[24] Through Heidegger, hermeneutics becomes capable of being either practical philosophy, as in our case, or speculative ontology.[25]

To understand Heidegger, at least in a basic way, one may take a simple sentence such as "The birds are singing." *Dasein* refers to the connection

---

18. Westphal, *Whose Community?*, 60–61.
19. Frankl, *The Will to Meaning*, 50–51.
20. Frankl, *The Will to Meaning*, 62–63; italics original.
21. Klemm, *Hermeneutical Inquiry*, vol. 1, 4.
22. Klemm, *Hermeneutical Inquiry*, vol. 1, 135.
23. Halling and Nill, "A Brief History," 8–10. The partly hidden nature of *Dasein* became a basis for understanding the unconscious among some psychotherapists.
24. Heidegger, *Being and Time*, 398–401.
25. Klemm, *Hermeneutical Inquiry*, vol. 1, 135; Klemm, *Hermeneutical Inquiry*, vol. 2, 83.

between the birds and the singing, as well as to the enactment of the connection—the act of singing itself. That is, the manner of being of the birds is enacted through singing. The process of connecting is accomplished through "existentials" referred to as understanding and mood. Understanding is a concrete phenomenon in space and time by which *Dasein* projects possibilities for itself in the world. A third existential is discourse—the structure of *Dasein* that allows experience to be intelligible and that is based on the openness of *Dasein* to the world, or the openness of being itself that makes possible the appearance of subjects and objects. *Dasein* encompasses both subject and object. That is, Heidegger attempts to bridge the subject-object divide. Language, much more than merely the expression of thought and feeling (understanding and mood), allows *Dasein* to be both subject and object, revealed and hidden, or, we might say, conscious and unconscious.[26] Hermeneutics, then, is not something that a reader might do, might apply to a text as an object; rather, it is characteristic of who the reader is.[27] It is an enactment of being of a reader.

The psychiatric theories most closely associated with Heidegger's thought are Ludwig Binswanger's *Daseinsanalyse* and Medard Boss's *Daseinsanalytik*, the former of which is considered a freer interpretation of Heidegger than the latter.[28] Frankl does not discuss Boss to any great extent, but supplements his argument for logotherapy by quoting Boss as saying, "Daseinsanalysis has nothing to do with psychotherapeutic practice."[29] Frankl further explains, "Logotherapy is concerned not only with being but also with meaning—not only with *ontos* but also with *logos*—and this feature may well account for the activistic, therapeutic orientation of logotherapy. In other words, logotherapy is not only analysis but also therapy."[30] It is because of this activistic orientation that this project can claim to be not only logotherapy, but also hermeneutics.

Binswanger, like Frankl, hoped to build a new psychiatric structure on the foundation of Freud's psychoanalysis and, also like Frankl, turned to

---

26. Klemm, *Hermeneutical Inquiry*, vol. 1, 136; Halling and Nill, "A Brief History," 9; Klemm, *Hermeneutical Inquiry*, vol. 2, 84.

27. Westphal, *Whose Community?*, 28 n. 3.

28. Halling and Nill, "A Brief History," 14–15; Spiegelberg, *Phenomenology in Psychology and Psychiatry*, 333 n.

29. Frankl, *Psychotherapy and Existentialism*, 134.

30. Frankl, *Psychotherapy and Existentialism*, 1.

philosophy to do so.³¹ His theory of *Daseinsanalyse* is described by Herbert Spiegelberg as "phenomenological anthropology."³² In essence, Binswanger was concerned with the inability of empirical science to confirm the existence of the unconscious. He hoped, therefore, to demonstrate its existence phenomenologically.³³ He believed that to understand a mental disorder the psychiatrist needed to not only understand the biology and the symptoms of the patient, but also the phenomenological worlds in which the patient lived.³⁴ Central to these worlds are the phenomena of freedom and love.³⁵

The difference between *Daseinsanalyse* and *Existenzanalyse* (logotherapy) is sharp for Frankl. The former is an analysis of being-in-the-world, a construct that replaces Freud's libido in Binswanger's thought.³⁶ The latter is an analysis of meaning in life. Frankl argues that his existential analysis surpasses *Daseinsanalyse* specifically because it leads to a concrete application, logotherapy, that *Daseinsanalyse* does not.³⁷ He states: "*Existenzanalyse* [Logotherapy] aims to complement these previous theories, to remodel and surpass them, and to complete a truer picture of the 'complete' man, namely, 'being man' as essentially spiritual *Existenz*."³⁸ Although Frankl is usually content to compare and contrast logotherapy with the theories of Freud and Adler, he does at least once include *Daseinsanalyse* along with psychoanalysis and individual psychology as theories having been complemented and completed by his own logotherapy and existential analysis.³⁹

---

31. Spiegelberg, *Phenomenology in Psychology and Psychiatry*, 200.
32. Spiegelberg, *Phenomenology in Psychology and Psychiatry*, 193.
33. Spiegelberg, *Phenomenology in Psychology and Psychiatry*, 218.
34. Binswanger, "The Existential Analysis School of Thought," 200–201.
35. Spiegelberg, *Phenomenology in Psychology and Psychiatry*, 219–20.
36. Binswanger, "The Existential Analysis School of Thought," 206.
37. Frankl, *The Feeling of Meaninglessness*, 81.
38. Frankl, *The Feeling of Meaninglessness*, 195.
39. Frankl, *The Feeling of Meaninglessness*, 194–95. The will to meaning is defined in contrast to the will to pleasure and the will to power in numerous places throughout Frankl's body of work with no reference to Binswanger. See, for example, Frankl, *The Will to Meaning*, 35 and numerous other places.

Edmund Husserl

Another common root for hermeneutics and Frankl is Edmund Husserl who intended his phenomenology to be a new starting point for philosophy, a method rigorous enough to challenge positivism—the view that only empirical science was a valid method of obtaining knowledge. When applied to empirical psychology, positivism is the belief that all mental processes can be explained by psychological laws in much the same way that the laws of physics explain the movement of objects. Husserl saw this position as a challenge to the existence of philosophy itself. He intended phenomenology to be a science of phenomena based on principles that allow meaning to be understood. Indeed, consciousness is understood not as a subjective experience, but as a process of being that is directed outward toward meanings, and that then transcends consciousness, reaching its realization through concrete expression.[40] His assertion of the "life world" as a prereflective world of lived experience became critical for the hermeneutics that followed and for Frankl.[41]

Indeed, the only definition of phenomenology that Frankl ever offered is based on Husserl's formulation. Frankl states: "Phenomenology, as I understand it, speaks the language of man's prereflective self-understanding rather than interpreting a given phenomenon after preconceived patterns."[42] Spiegelberg argues that phenomenology allowed Frankl to free himself from the preconceived patterns of psychoanalysis and individual psychology. Consequently, Frankl was able to develop logotherapy by hearing his patients instead of offering them interpretations.[43] As such, Frankl was not interested in phenomenology *per se*, but rather, in its application to psychiatry.[44] For example, Frankl bases his three assumptions of logotherapy (freedom of the will, the will to meaning, and meaning in life) on his understanding of phenomenology, that is to say, by recognizing these phenomena as expressed by his patients.[45]

---

40. Klemm, *Hermeneutical Inquiry*, vol. 2, 56–57.

41. Klemm, *Hermeneutical Inquiry*, vol. 2, 179–80; Frankl, *Psychotherapy and Existentialism*, 2, note 2.

42. Frankl, *Psychotherapy and Existentialism*, 2 n. 2; Frankl, *The Feeling of Meaninglessness*, 108.

43. Spiegelberg, *Phenomenology in Psychology and Psychiatry*, 353.

44. Spiegelberg, *Phenomenology in Psychology and Psychiatry*, 245, 352.

45. Frankl, *Psychotherapy and Existentialism*, 2, 11, 14.

Husserl's phenomenology entered the field of psychiatry, and strongly influenced Frankl, largely through the work of Max Scheler.[46] In writing about his final days of association with the Society for Individual Psychology, Frankl states: "At that time I finally saw through my own psychologism. My ultimate shakeup came from Max Scheler whose *Formalismus in der Ethik* [*Formalism in Ethics*] I carried with me like a bible."[47] The influence of Scheler on Frankl may best be seen in Frankl's concept of dimensional ontology and in the development of his categorical values.

Frankl gives partial credit to Scheler for inspiring his dimensional ontology—Frankl's conception of the human person that includes a noetic, spiritual core.[48] Scheler's influence is in his stratification of feeling based on the vital, the mental, and the spiritual. Each stratification has its own relationship to values.[49] Scheler explains, "A *spiritual* level also exists for this analysis, one that has nothing to do with the sphere of the sensible or the sphere of the vital or of the lived body, which is to be sharply distinguished from the sensible sphere."[50] Frankl draws from this the notion of a spiritual layer separate from the layers of mind and body, but unlike Scheler, speaks of "dimensions" rather than "layers" as a way to emphasize the unity of the human person.[51]

Spiegelberg notes that while Frankl's categorical values are original to Frankl, they do owe some degree of dependence on Scheler.[52] By use of his stratification system, Scheler allows for value hierarchies to be deliberately considered.[53] He explains, "In the *totality* of the realm of values there exists a singular order, an '*order of ranks*' that all values possess among themselves. It is because of this that a value is '*higher*' or '*lower*' than another one. This order lies in the essence of values themselves."[54] Frankl states: "The rank of a value is experienced together with the value itself. In other words,

---

46. Spiegelberg, *Phenomenology in Psychology and Psychiatry*, 16, 348, 352.
47. Frankl, *Recollections*, 62.
48. Frankl, *The Will the Meaning*, 22.
49. Spiegelberg, *Phenomenology in Psychology and Psychiatry*, 17.
50. Scheler, *Formalism in Ethics*, 65; italics original.
51. Frankl, *The Will to Meaning*, 22.
52. Spiegelberg, *Phenomenology in Psychology and Psychiatry*, 351–52.
53. Spiegleberg, *Phenomenology in Psychology and Psychiatry*, 17.
54. Scheler, *Formalism in Ethics*, 86–87; italics original.

the experience of one value includes the experience that it ranks higher than another. There is no place for value conflicts."⁵⁵

For both Scheler and Frankl, values must be lived. Scheler explains, "It is not only in 'inner perception'... but also in the felt and lived affair with *world*... in the course of *performing* such intentional functions and acts, that values and their order flash before us!... A spirit limited to perception and thinking would be absolutely *blind* to values."⁵⁶ Frankl, likewise, explains, "However, the experience of the hierarchical order of values does not dispel man from decision making. Man is pushed by drives. But he is pulled by values. He is always free to accept or to reject a value he is offered by a situation."⁵⁷

Hans-Georg Gadamer

The central argument of Hans-Georg Gadamer is that the use of any hermeneutical method obscures an original experience of the wholeness of life, or an appearance of what he calls "truth in being." "There is a saying of Heraclitus," writes Gadamer, "The *logos* is common to all, but people behave as if each had a private reason. Does this have to remain this way?"⁵⁸ His philosophy asserts that human belongingness to the truth of being may be seen through art, history, and language; indeed the very concept of a method implies an alienation from the text for Gadamer. He explains that method must be held secondary to the experience of the world. For example, when a work of art reveals something true about everyday life that was previously hidden, a basic understanding of truth in experience has occurred that underlies any method of interpretation.⁵⁹ A work of art may even reveal something unexpected to the artist. According to Gadamer, "Works of art are detached from their origins and, just because of this, begin to speak—perhaps *surprising even their creators*."⁶⁰ In other words,

---

55. Frankl, *The Will to Meaning*, 57.
56. Scheler, *Formalism in Ethics*, 68; italics original.
57. Frankl, *The Will to Meaning*, 57.
58. Gadamer, "What is Practice?," 252.
59. Klemm, *Hermeneutical Inquiry*, vol. 2, 174–77.
60. Gadamer, "Hermeneutics and Logocentrism," 123, quoted in Westphal, *Whose Community?*, 80. Westphal's italics.

works of art, including texts, are "understood not as objects to be observed and explained but as voices to be listened to."[61]

Therefore, when the Book of Job reveals something that the reader perceives as a truth about life, understanding of that truth comes before the application of a hermeneutic or method. A logotherapy hermeneutic, therefore, could be understood as a way of making sense of the truth that was understood. Consequently, it remains secondary. This will ensure that a logotherapy hermeneutic will remain what Klemm calls practical philosophy rather than imposing its own understanding on the text. To explain this point in greater detail, Gadamer gives examples of the aesthetic consciousness, the historic consciousness, and the hermeneutical consciousness. He explains hermeneutics by giving examples of alienation such as the experience of art that may speak to us, or not, independent of art criticism, or such as the problem of developing an historical method not tied to the concerns of the time in which it is produced. The task of hermeneutics is to overcome the alienations and misunderstandings in the aesthetic, historical, and hermeneutic consciousnesses.[62]

However, Gadamer does not see the question of hermeneutics as confined to these areas, but rather as universal—including areas such as the meaning of concepts such as "theory" and "practice" integral to his understanding of hermeneutics as practical philosophy.[63] The primary domain of hermeneutics is to find the words needed to reach and understand another person.[64] He explains, "That is the fundamental dimension of hermeneutics. Genuine speaking, which has something to say and hence does not give prearranged signals, but rather seeks words through which one reaches the other person, is the universal human task."[65]

Understanding for Gadamer is identified with interpretation. This means that linguistic prejudgments—logotherapy in this case—both determine who we are and allow us to enter into dialogue. Indeed, dialogue would not be possible without them. Yet, the occasion of dialogue "reads" prejudgments as much as prejudgments influence the reading of the text.[66]

---

61. Westphal, *Whose Community?*, 89.

62. Gadamer, "The Universality of the Hermeneutic Problem," 179–82.

63. Gadamer, "What is Practice?," 241–42; Klemm, *Hermeneutical Inquiry*, vol. 2, 235–36, 246, 248.

64. Gadamer, "The Universality of the Hermeneutic Problem," 185, 189.

65. Gadamer, "The Universality of the Hermeneutic Problem," 189.

66. Klemm, *Hermeneutical Inquiry*, vol. 2, 236.

As Westphal puts it, "All interpretation is relative to traditions that have formed the perspectives and presuppositions that guide it."[67] Understanding is also further identified with application, that is, the process of making understanding concrete.[68] Understanding serves to actualize meaning wherein universal meaning and specific dialogue codetermine each other.[69] Therefore, the vocabulary of logotherapy can be properly understood as a hermeneutic. It is the vocabulary by which the logotherapy reader enters into dialogue with the text and realizes meaning.

Gadamer is careful to point out, however, that the meaning realized is not arbitrarily imposed by the reader. The text has its own unique being with which a reader comes into dialogue, and this unique being is expressed anew with each reader. Gadamer explains that a text "if it is to be understood properly . . . must be understood at every moment, in every particular situation, in a new and different way."[70] This accords well with what Frankl understands of meaning. He writes, "Meaning is relative in that it is related to a specific person who is entangled in a specific situation. One could say that it differs first from man to man and second from day to day, indeed, hour to hour."[71] Therefore, the responsibility of a logotherapy hermeneutic is to realize meaning in the Book of Job through logotherapy's particular situation.

Paul Ricoeur

Another significant thinker whose work informs the development of a logotherapy hermeneutic is Paul Ricoeur. Ricoeur, the French translator of Husserl, finds an affinity between phenomenology and hermeneutics. Indeed, he flatly states, "Hermeneutics is erected on the basis of phenomenology and thus preserves something of the philosophy from which it nevertheless differs: *phenomenology remains the unsurpassable presupposition of hermeneutics.*"[72] Ricoeur believes that every act of self-reflection is already interpretation; that is, the self interprets the meaning of its being through its actions and interactions in the world. Both Frankl and Ricoeur

---

67. Westphal, *Whose Community?*, 71.
68. Westphal, *Whose Community?*, 108–9.
69. Klemm, *Hermeneutical Inquiry*, vol. 2, 236.
70. Gadamer, *Truth and Method*, 275.
71. Frankl, *The Will to Meaning*, 54.
72. Ricoeur, *Hermeneutics and the Human Sciences*, 101; italics original.

stress that the question of meaning is primary and is realized concretely.[73] Ricoeur states that "the central question of phenomenology must be recognized as a question about meaning... *The choice in favor of meaning is thus the most general presupposition of any hermeneutics.*"[74] He explains further, "The most fundamental phenomenological presupposition of a philosophy of interpretation is that every question concerning any sort of 'being' [*étant*] is a question about the meaning of that 'being.'"[75] In other words, like logotherapy, Ricoeur is concerned not only with being, but also with meaning, and especially with meaning as realized concretely in the world.

Ricoeur additionally critiques what he sees as the idealistic form of phenomenology developed by Husserl. By this idealism, he refers to the position that an absolute self, or "I," exists beyond the actions of the self in space and time.[76] This critique is necessary according to Ricoeur to allow dialogue between hermeneutics and phenomenology.[77] He explains, "If all meaning is for a consciousness, then no consciousness is self-consciousness before being conscious *of* something *toward which* it surpasses itself."[78] Frankl likewise moves logotherapy in this direction, without going as far, perhaps, as Ricoeur, when he states, "Being human is directed to something other than itself."[79] Frankl explains, "One must recognize that being human profoundly means being engaged and entangled in a situation," and, further, that the "tension is ... between reality and ideal, between being and meaning."[80]

Ricoeur seeks to ground hermeneutics within phenomenology by way of what he calls a "long route" in comparison to Heidegger's "short route." He sees this effort as complementary to Heidegger's path rather than contrary. The "short route" refers to Heidegger's ontology of understanding, that is, the reversal of the hermeneutic question from the meaning of the text to the nature of the being capable of questioning and understanding. Ricoeur accepts this reversal, but does not believe that it makes earlier (that

---

73. Thompson, "Introduction," 21; Klemm, *Hermeneutical Inquiry*, vol. 1, 225.

74. Ricoeur, *Hermeneutics and the Human Sciences*, 114; italics original.

75. Ricoeur, *Hermeneutics and the Human Sciences*, 114. This is also Heidegger's question in *Being and Time*.

76. Klemm, *Hermeneutical Inquiry*, vol. 1, 226.

77. Ricoeur, *Hermeneutics and the Human Sciences*, 105.

78. Ricoeur, *Hermeneutics and the Human Sciences*, 115; italics original.

79. Frankl, *The Will to Meaning*, 50.

80. Frankl, *The Will to Meaning*, 51.

is to say, modern-empirical) problems vanish.[81] His "long route" involves using Husserl's phenomenology of language as a way of connecting the modern problems of hermeneutics with the postmodern understanding of being. In other words, where Heidegger uses an understanding of ontology, Ricoeur uses an analysis of linguistics and semantics. In short, he addresses what were originally empirical problems through phenomenology. For Ricoeur, this saves Heidegger's thought from becoming disconnected from the mainstream and provides postmodern hermeneutics with grounding in phenomenology.[82] That is to say, Ricoeur takes modern-empirical questions seriously and seeks to answer them with deliberation from the point of view of a postmodern understanding of the use of language.

Because of this, Ricoeur believes that objective strategies for interpretation—psychoanalysis being a notable example—are not incompatible with hermeneutics especially when hermeneutics is thought of as practical philosophy. He supports this view by demonstrating that language has both an objective sense as well as an existential appropriation neither of which may be reduced to the other.[83] He privileges the text over the spoken word inasmuch as the text is fixed. Reading replaces dialogue with an absent author. However, the question is not what the author intended to say at all; the question is what the text wants to say, right now, to this reader.[84] More specifically, the question for a logotherapy hermeneutic is what the text wants to say to a reader informed by logotherapy. The text will question logotherapy to discover meaning. From Ricoeur's point of view, the privilege given to text over the spoken word suggests that a logotherapy hermeneutic is an even better dialogue partner with a text than a logotherapist (or psychoanalyst) is with a patient speaking a narrative in a logotherapy (or psychoanalytic) session.

Moreover, Ricoeur believes that the simple dichotomy between interpretation (the domain of the natural sciences, including historical-criticism) and understanding (the domain of the human sciences, including logotherapy) has become obsolete. Rather, he sees these as two different kinds of reading and as two different attitudes that engage each other in dialogue.[85] This dialogue is the way that hermeneutics grounded in phe-

81. Ricoeur, "Existence and Hermeneutics," 187–90.
82. Klemm, *Hermeneutical Inquiry*, vol. 2, 179–80.
83. Klemm, *Hermeneutical Inquiry*, vol. 1, 228–29.
84. Ricoeur, "What Is a Text?," 234, 244.
85. Ricoeur, "What Is a Text?," 233, 236.

nomenology can address what were once modern-empirical questions. Ricoeur explains, "Reading is like the performance of a musical score: it betokens the fulfillment, the actualization of the semantic virtualities of the text."[86] At the same time, this performance takes place within a world that "the text discloses in front of itself."[87] This means that logotherapy cannot simply read itself into a text, but must remain open to receive from the text as well. That is, to paraphrase Ricoeur and Frankl as quoted above, the logotherapy reader is directed toward a text that presents its own references to reality.[88]

SUMMARY OF A LOGOTHERAPY HERMENEUTIC

For purposes of clarification, Frankl finds it helpful to compare logotherapy to the (then) dominant schools of thought in psychiatry. Although contemporary biblical studies has in the last 40 years seen an influx of newer methodologies and reading strategies, it is still nonetheless dominated by historical-critical concerns. Therefore, it may be helpful to consider the ways in which a logotherapy hermeneutic differs from the historical-critical approach. John Barton identifies four characteristics of the historical-critical approach: genetic questioning, original meaning, historical reconstruction, and disinterested scholarship.[89] The Book of Job may have, and almost certainly does have, many layers of composition. While this historical-critical matter will inform a logotherapy hermeneutic, it is not the focus of our hermeneutic; a logotherapy hermeneutic will be based on how a reader informed by logotherapy discovers meaning in the text as it now exists. This parallels the relationship between logotherapy and the empirical sciences. Just as logotherapy may be informed by a finding of biology, it retains its focus on the personal discovery of meaning.

Whereas historical-criticism requires a degree of reductionism, say to reveal an historical point about composition, a logotherapy hermeneutic will avoid reductionism because it seeks to realize its insights in the living understanding of the text. This follows from its desire to be true to the existential-phenomenological tradition that Frankl uses to develop

---

86. Ricoeur, "What Is a Text?," 242.

87. Ricoeur, *Hermeneutics and the Human Sciences*, 192.

88. For an example of Ricoeur's hermeneutic applied to a portion of the Book of Job, see LaCocque, "Impotence of Religion and Philosophy," 33–52.

89. Barton, *The Cambridge Companion to Biblical Interpretation*, 9–12.

logotherapy. Therefore, a logotherapy hermeneutic will remain practical philosophy in the sense described by Klemm, as well as a relativistic hermeneutic in the sense described by Westphal; that is, one based on the defined position of logotherapy, one that will remain true to the concept of dialogue between the logotherapy reader and the text. Moreover, it will not reduce the text to the mere illustration of a point about logotherapy, a tendency found in some earlier attempts at logotherapy readings of texts.[90]

A logotherapy hermeneutic will also avoid psychologism in that it will not try to guess at an author's intention as some historical-critical and psychological readings attempt. A world presented by a text will be seen as similar to a human social world; both offer possibilities for understanding, but not a static structure to be dissected. An attempt to reduce either to a closed system is to lose rather than to gain understanding.[91] Thus, a logotherapy hermeneutic is an enactment of meaning for the reader; it is a concrete phenomenon that occurs in space and time between the logotherapy reader and the text. Unlike logotherapy, other forms of existential analysis derived from the existential-phenomenological tradition lack this concrete application that logotherapy makes possible.

A logotherapy hermeneutic, moreover, will make use of the distinction between literal discourse and figurative discourse. The former carries a single meaning; empirical scientific discourse is the premier example. The latter carries multiple meanings and may create new meanings. Poetry, such as found in the Book of Job, is an example of the latter.[92] For instance, Job 28:3 reads: "Men put an end to darkness and to every farthest limit. They search out ore in gloom and deep darkness." A logotherapy hermeneutic will emphasize the multiple meanings of these poetic words. Indeed, along with Ricoeur, a logotherapy hermeneutic asserts that hermeneutics is properly defined by those expressions that carry a double meaning. Interpretation is the work of discovering the hidden meaning within the literal meaning.[93]

---

90. See, for example, Atlas, "Logotherapy and the Book of Job," 29–33; and Leslie, *Jesus and Logotherapy*, 7.

91. Klemm, *Hermeneutical Inquiry*, vol. 2, 91.

92. Klemm, *Hermeneutical Inquiry*, vol. 1, 229.

93. Ricoeur, "Existence and Hermeneutics," 192–93.

APPLICATION OF A LOGOTHERAPY HERMENEUTIC

Just as Frankl freed himself from the preconceived patterns of other systems of psychology, a logotherapy hermeneutic enables discovered meaning to be unique.[94] In doing so, a logotherapy hermeneutic will employ the framework of logotherapy that Frankl derived from listening to his patients. This means it will listen for expressions of the loss of meaning that Frankl calls the existential vacuum. It will be sensitive to expressions of Frankl's primary assumptions, such as the will to meaning, reflected in the way the text seeks to overcome the existential vacuum. It will look for examples of the categorical values—the creative, experiential, and attitudinal ways in which meaning is actively discovered. A logotherapy hermeneutic will explore the meaning of freedom and responsibility as the reader challenges her own existential vacuum through engaging in dialogue with the text. When applied to the Book of Job, a logotherapy hermeneutic uses Frankl's vocabulary of suffering—a vocabulary that many suffering persons understand—to explore a text concerned with suffering.

As we apply this hermeneutic to the Book of Job in the following chapters, three central movements or themes emerge based on their resonance with the vocabulary of logotherapy. The first movement or theme relates to the existential vacuum and the discovery of meaning in the face of it. This theme is prominent from chapters 1 to 27. Included in this rather large section is the prose prologue of chapters 1 and 2 wherein Job suffers loss. Chapter 3 begins the poetic section of Job; in this chapter Job expresses the turmoil of his suffering. Chapter 4 begins the dialogue between Job and his friends that runs through the end of this movement.

The second movement or theme encompasses chapters 28 to 37. The prominent logotherapy principle emerging from our reading of these chapters is the will to meaning. Meaning is found to function for logotherapy in a way somewhat similar to wisdom in the Book of Job. Chapter 28 is recognized as a wisdom poem. Chapters 29 to 31 comprise a monologue of Job. In chapters 32 to 37, Elihu delivers another monologue that concludes with wisdom imagery.

The third and final movement begins with the God speeches found in chapters 38 to 41. Job makes his final response to God in 42:5–6 that concludes the poetic section of the book. The prose epilogue concludes the book with the remainder of chapter 42. The theme that emerges here

---

94. Klemm, *Hermeneutical Inquiry*, vol. 2, 61–62.

is that of transcendence as understood in the vocabulary of logotherapy, especially transcendence as it relates to the possibility of ultimate meaning.

We now apply a logotherapy hermeneutic to the first movement.

4

Job and Frankl's Existential Vacuum

RECALL THAT AMONG CONTEMPORARY biblical scholars, it was especially Newsom, Boss, and Cox who underscored the existential quality of the Book of Job. Their work both grounds and warrants our effort to bring Frankl's existential approach into dialogue with that biblical text. Consequently, they emerge as our primary dialogue partners in applying a logotherapy hermeneutic to Job. Boss, for instance, states, "If what Job is saying is about a question, it is not a theoretical question, but an existential one."[1] Cox calls what Job is saying "the absurd."[2] Newsom drives the point home by bringing Philippe Nemo into the discussion, a thinker who understands Job's situation specifically in terms of Heideggerian *Angst*.[3] Newsom writes, "The intentionality of human existence, which expresses itself in projects and relationships and gives to life a sense of coherency, has been shattered for Job. All that remains is turmoil—incessant and emotionally charged events without coherent meaning—from which misery only death can provide relief."[4] Newsom sounds like a logotherapist in this sentence. One could rewrite her sentence with Frankl's vocabulary: "The area of freedom in human existence, which expresses itself in the creative and experiential values and gives to life a sense of meaning, has been shattered for Job. All that

---

1. Boss, *Human Consciousness of God*, 35.
2. Cox, *The Triumph of Impotence*, 23–24.
3. Nemo, *Job and the Excess of Evil*, 107–11; see, also, Newsom, *The Book of Job*, 96.
4. Newsom, *The Book of Job*, 96.

remains is existential vacuum—incessant and emotionally charged events without coherent meaning."

"What is at stake is not individual hypocrisy or venality, but the very meaning of the concept of piety," writes Newsom.[5] The satan, representing a hermeneutic of suspicion, has unmasked a contradiction that "when brought to light, threatens to undermine a fundamental category" of religious discourse.[6] That is to say, the satan has unmasked the question of disinterested piety. Is it possible for the human person to be "whole and upright," to live an integrated and meaningful life, in a world without reward for such a life, in a world of unjust suffering that even God in the Book of Job calls "without purpose" (2:3)? For Newsom, the interest "lies in how Job will articulate a form of piety that persuasively resolves the threat of incoherency"—the existential vacuum—unmasked by the satan.[7]

In addition, Newsom, Boss, and Cox all assert that the problem of Job is a universal human problem. Newsom writes, "A single human being's experience is framed within the common condition of humanity."[8] Boss asserts "the book of Job tells of various faces of God that the consciousness of humankind may encounter."[9] Cox states, "Job is no longer merely a man with a problem . . . he is also, and more essentially, a type, and his condition is a typical condition."[10] Cox draws attention to the fact that Job lacks specifics that identify him as belonging to any specific place or time. "No matter who reads him he can recognize a shared experience," says Cox. "He does not lie in Jerusalem or in Hebron, but squats on an anonymous pile of detritus outside any town at all . . . Job suffers precisely because he is subject to the common lot of humanity."[11] For Cox, the existential vacuum in Job becomes a "clear starting point for further analysis of what makes man function."[12]

---

5. Newsom, *The Book of Job*, 55.

6. Newsom, *The Book of Job*, 56. Recall that the satan is written throughout with the definite article and in lower case letters to indicate that the word is used as a description of function (accuser/adversary) and not as the ontological source of evil that develops in later tradition as essentially all commentators note, for example, see Habel, *The Book of Job*, 89.

7. Newsom, *The Book of Job*, 56.

8. Newsom, *The Book of Job*, 57.

9. Boss, *Human Consciousness of God*, 12.

10. Cox, *The Triumph of Impotence*, 51.

11. Cox, *The Triumph of Impotence*, 52.

12. Cox, *The Triumph of Impotence*, 52.

THE PROLOGUE (JOB 1:1—2:13): A MEANINGFUL LIFE

The first thing we learn about Job is that he is "whole and upright" (1:1). These two words, תם וישר, taken together are used to describe Noah, Abraham, and Jacob. The Hebrew word תם that I translate "whole" is translated "blameless" in the Revised Standard Version (RSV). Habel notes it is from the same root as ובתמתו "in his integrity" found in 2:3 and 2:9. He sees them as foreshadowing later developments and thus serve to tie the prologue to the remainder of the book.[13] Hartley notes that the word תם refers to personal integrity when applied to a human person and to the spotlessness of an animal selected for sacrifice.[14] "Whole" seems to me to be a closer parallel to "integrity" than does "blameless" because both English words convey a sense of completeness. The implication is that Job's life is complete or well-integrated. In logotherapy, a complete or well-integrated life is one in which a sense of meaning and purpose prevails.

Logotherapy defines a meaningful life as one in which the categorical values—Frankl's creative, experiential, and attitudinal values—are realized to the highest degree possible. In the prologue we find that Job does, in fact, realize each of these values. His attitudinal value is stated in 1:1 where we read that Job "feared Elohim and turned aside from evil." Job's creative value, the result of his work, is implied in 1:3 where it says, "And his herd was seven thousand sheep and three thousand camels and five hundred yoke of oxen and five hundred female donkeys and very many slaves." Newsom reminds us that these symbolic numbers, adding to a multiple of ten, serve to signify the wholeness, the integrity, of Job's world.[15] Verses 4 and 5 explain Job's experiential value as reflected in his religious observance. In verse 5 we read, "And he arose early in the morning and offered burnt offerings in the number for all, for Job said, 'Perchance my sons have sinned and cursed Elohim in their minds.' Thus Job did everyday."

The "very many slaves" are taken as a literary device to indicate Job's great wealth. If one wishes to consider the relationship of justice to meaning, however, it is beneficial to recall that Frankl himself was enslaved for 2 years and 7 months. "I was Number 119,104," Frankl writes, "and most of the time I was digging and laying tracks for railway lines. At one time,

---

13. Habel, *The Book of Job*, 83.
14. Hartley, *The Book of Job*, 67.
15. Newsom, *The Book of Job*, 53.

my job was to dig a tunnel, without help, for a water main under a road."[16] Logotherapy recognizes that the "area of freedom" is variable and is often restricted, such as by terminal illness, imprisonment, enslavement, and, ultimately, by death itself. In spite of his experiences, Frankl writes "life is potentially meaningful under any conditions, even those which are most miserable."[17] Therefore, justice is not held by logotherapy to be a necessary condition for meaning. Logotherapy asserts that the lives of Job's slaves were potentially just as meaningful as Job's.

Our logotherapy hermeneutic sees meaning well fulfilled in 1:1–5. The reader soon finds out, however, that this condition exists because God has "put a hedge" around Job and his blessings, protecting him from loss. Boss refers to this situation as a closed system wherein God is seen as nurturing.[18] This issue is presented by the satan in 1:9–11, "Does Job fear Elohim for nothing? . . . But indeed, I pray, extend your hand and touch all that is his and he will certainly curse you to your face." The satan's challenge becomes the measure of disinterested piety; Job's piety will be considered genuine only if he decides not to curse God. For logotherapy, issues of reductionism and nihilism are raised by the satan's challenge.

The first wave of tragedy strikes Job when his blessings—his property and his children—are suddenly removed. His initial attitudinal value, that is, the stand taken toward unavoidable suffering, is recorded in 1:21, "Yahweh has given and Yahweh has seized; the Name of Yahweh be blessed." Job's first answer to the satan's challenge is clear. He is choosing to bless the Name of Yahweh despite these losses. He has certainly not cursed God. His body and life remain sound, suggesting that future blessings may be obtained just as they were before. That is to say, Job still possesses the means to realize the creative and experiential values through his body and his life (his health). Job does not express any concern that these values will not remain future possibilities. For this reason, we may wonder, along with the satan, if this represents the authentic Job.

Scheler proposes levels of feeling based on the degree to which they can be influenced by outside forces. This view influences Frankl's dimensional ontology. It is unclear to the reader, and, as the reader soon learns, to the satan, if Job's first response represents his deepest, authentic self (the noetic dimension) or merely his psychological self (the mind-body

---

16. Frankl, *Man's Search for Meaning*, 7.
17. Frankl, *Man's Search for Meaning*, 137.
18. Boss, *Human Consciousness of God*, 22.

dimension). From the logotherapy point of view, the question of Job's piety can only be answered from the noetic dimension.[19]

In logotherapy, there is a connection between the well-being of the body and the potential for meaning that derives from the creative and experiential values. Job references his body in 1:21 where a reasonable translation may be, "Naked I came from my mother's womb and naked I shall return [to the tomb]."[20] Newsom provides support for this understanding when she writes, "The metaphor with which Job comprehended his situation in the first episode drew upon imagery of the body's nakedness, and thus highlighted the intimate relationship between body and meaning."[21] The connection is reinforced by understanding the "coming forth" from the womb and the "returning" to the tomb as the "giving" and "taking" of Yahweh described by Job.[22] As Samuel Terrien and Paul Scherer have noted, as late as 1954 this precise Joban formula was still in use in funeral rituals in northwest Saudi Arabia. The survivors of the deceased ritually recite, "His Lord gave him; his Lord has taken him away."[23]

The second test strikes Job's body, placing the future realization of creative and experiential values in jeopardy. Nevertheless, Job continues to exercise the attitudinal value; he may not explicitly bless God, but he continues to refuse to utter a curse: "We have been receiving good from Elohim, but shall we not receive evil?" (2:10). From the point of view of logotherapy, Job continues to recognize meaning in his life by his choice of response. Frankl writes that "life never ceases to hold a meaning, for even a person deprived of both creative and experiential values is still challenged by a meaning to fulfill, that is, by the meaning inherent in the right, in an upright way of suffering."[24] This upright way of suffering means to hold fast to one's humanity.

The words of the satan in 1:9–11 and the words of Job's wife in 2:9b are suggestive, however, that Job is tempted to abandon his humanity to nihilism and reductionism. As noted earlier, logotherapy works specifically

---

19. See Scheler, *Formalism in Ethics*, 337.

20. Here "[to the tomb]" is used as a translation for the word שמה meaning "There," understood as a term for the underworld. It is set in parallel with "mother's womb" because the underworld is understood as the "womb" of Mother Earth. See Habel, *The Book of Job*, 93.

21. Newsom, *The Book of Job*, 59.

22. Newsom, *The Book of Job*, 59.

23. Terrien and Scherer, "The Book of Job," 917.

24. Frankl, *The Will to Meaning*, 70.

to counter nihilism and reductionism, positions Frankl sees as partly responsible for the Holocaust. Frankl considers reductionism, moreover, to be the contemporary expression of nihilism. For logotherapy, any attempt to narrate human psychology in less than human terms renders human choice meaningless.[25] Frankl writes, "There is a danger that we may corrupt a man, that we may work into the hands of his Nihilism . . . if we present him with a concept of man which is not the true concept of man."[26] Frankl explains that a false concept of the human person is advanced "wherever we present man as an automaton of reflexes, as a mind-machine, or as a bundle of instincts, as a pawn of drives and reactions, as a mere product of instinct, inheritance, and environment."[27]

This very attempt at reductionism has been implicit in the satan's challenge from the beginning. When the satan implies in 1:9–11 that Job's motivation for piety is the hedge of protection God has put around him, a mere function of what he has—wealth, family, religion—the satan is saying in effect that Job's actions and attitude are the result of that environment or that situation. This, we have just seen, is what logotherapy considers a false concept of the human person. The position of nihilism is represented by Job's wife who appears in 2:9b and says, "Do you still hold fast to your integrity? Curse God and die." From the viewpoint of logotherapy, if Job abandons a sense of meaning (abandons his integrity, succumbs to nihilism) only because the means by which meaning may be realized (the creative and experiential values) have been removed, then Job would be responding as an automaton, not as a human being. The attitudinal value is recognized as being of a different nature than the creative and experiential values for it can never be taken from a person; it always allows the person to retain her humanity. For Frankl's logotherapy "man is by no means a product of inheritance and environment. Man ultimately decides for himself!"[28]

Newsom also argues that the satan's hermeneutic of suspicion is reductionist. That is, the satan claims to know Job's motivation for his integrity when it is not at all clear that even Job himself knows it. As Newsom puts it, "Both God and *hassatan* seek to narrate Job." She continues, "They are equally certain that they know the truth about him and that they can state it in a single sentence. The violence that will erupt upon Job is

25. Frankl, *The Feeling of Meaninglessness*, 219–20.
26. Frankl, *The Feeling of Meaninglessness*, 219.
27. Frankl, *The Feeling of Meaninglessness*, 219.
28. Frankl, *The Feeling of Meaninglessness*, 218.

already anticipated in the violence done in these attempts to define him."²⁹ For Newsom, the genre of the prologue bespeaks this type of reductionist knowledge, wherein defining the truth about Job is the highest value. Ambiguity cannot be tolerated. Newsom illustrates this by having us imagine God responding to the satan with the words, "Well, I don't think you are right. But I guess we will never know."³⁰ Once the need to define Job's motivation is established, everything is permitted. Newsom even implicates the reader. To the extent that the reader also wishes to answer the question, she who turns the page is "not so different from God who says, 'Very well, he is in your hands'" (2:6a).³¹

Newsom provides additional support for logotherapy's view that Job's wife represents nihilism. Concerning Job's wife, she writes, "The nihilism of the position she and *hassatan* embrace is evident from the one word in her speech that is not an implicit quotation of the heavenly voices: 'Die.'"³² Newsom goes on to explain the position held by Job's wife, and also by the satan, is a position incapable of sustaining life in the midst of catastrophe.³³ Logotherapy would add that it is a position incapable of sustaining life under any condition.³⁴

"In all this," the text tells us in 2:10, "Job did not sin with his lips." We have previously mentioned the question of whether Job may have sinned in his mind. That this is a possibility recognized in the Book of Job is present in 1:5 wherein Job offers burnt offerings for his children, "For Job said, 'Perhaps my sons sinned and cursed Elohim in their minds.'" Clearly, 2:10 does not say that Job cursed God in his mind. Logotherapy resonates with Newsom's reading of Job's second response. She sees it as an example of "radical acceptance," a term for which she cites Dorothee Soelle, and that

29. Newsom, *The Book of Job*, 68; italics original.
30. Newsom, *The Book of Job*, 68.
31. Newsom, *The Book of Job*, 69.
32. Newsom, *The Book of Job*, 60; italics original.
33. Newsom, *The Book of Job*, 60.
34. In the history of interpretation, the figure of Job's wife, a minor character, has taken up an inordinate amount of interpretive energy. Augustine considered her to be an unwitting ally of the satan, and, it must be admitted, associating her with nihilism is not any more sympathetic. Feminist writers have read against this interpretation. Psychological interpretations have seen the character as representative of Job's own unconscious and, thus, represents an image of internal deliberation on the part of Job. For more on interpretation, see Habel, *The Book of Job*, 96, among others. For psychological interpretations, see Boss, *Human Consciousness of God*, 31; and Cox, *The Triumph of Impotence*, 36–37, among others.

she defines as "a stance that recognizes the unavoidability of certain suffering and chooses not to flee from it."[35] She also asserts that radical acceptance is the alternative to nihilism.[36] Job has rejected nihilism at the end of the prologue, as Newsom puts it, "the principle of retribution quite literally has no place in Job's moral imagination (to the chagrin of *hassatan*).[37]

THE TURMOIL OF JOB (JOB 3:1–26): JOB IN THE EXISTENTIAL VACUUM

"I am not at ease nor am I quiet. I have no rest, but turmoil comes." In 3:26, Job names his psychological state רגז—a noun that means turmoil, agitation, raging, wrath. The root verb means to quiver or quake. Hartley notes that the word is set in opposition to נחתי, a word with the connotation of mental rest; it can, therefore, be understood as describing "the agitated state that results from complete lack of peace."[38] Newsom notes that the word means shaking when applied to inanimate objects and when applied to living beings refers to "intense emotional agitation."[39] The word carries more weight when considered within the overall context of chapter 3, as we will see. This is because, as Newsom notes, turmoil "is to the order of lived experience as chaos is to the cosmic order."[40]

In logotherapy, such a state of emotional turmoil is called noogenic neurosis if it is the result of existential vacuum; that is to say, when it is based on a sense of meaninglessness.[41] Job did not abandon himself to reductionism and nihilism; he retained meaning through the exercise of the attitudinal value. Yet, his suffering continues. It is described by God in 2:3 as suffering חנם . This word expresses the sense of meaninglessness. It is often translated as "in vain," "for nothing," or "for no purpose." Therefore, the turmoil that results from such suffering is understood by logotherapy to be noogenic, that is to say, the result of existential vacuum.

---

35. Newsom, *The Book of Job*, 60.
36. Newsom, *The Book of Job*, 60–61.
37. Newsom, *The Book of Job*, 64; italics original.
38. Hartley, *The Book of Job*, 100.
39. Newsom, *The Book of Job*, 94.
40. Newsom, *The Book of Job*, 94.
41. Frankl, *The Will to Meaning*, 85; Frankl, *On the Theory and Therapy*, 161–62. If emotional distress is the result of psychological or physical disturbances, Frankl uses the terms psychogenic or somatogenic, respectively.

According to Frankl, the existential vacuum is a loss of meaning orientation, a loss of recognized meaning and purpose. This may come about when previous values, be they creative or experiential, no longer provide a sense of meaning.[42] Frankl describes the existential vacuum not only as "the expression of a sense of meaninglessness, or of that inner emptiness and void," but also as an "abyss-experience."[43] Job expresses the depth of this abyss-experience in 3:20–26. "Why is light given to him that is in misery," Job asks in verses 20–21, "and life to those bitter in soul who long for death but it does not come, and dig for it more than for hidden treasures?" This verse makes an interesting parallel with chapter 28 that describes wisdom as being sought like precious metals and jewels. Job's experience in chapter 3 appears in this light to be the inverse of the experience described in chapter 28.

We are not alone in asserting that 3:20–26 describe a condition that can be understood in terms of the existential vacuum, a notion based on Heideggerian *Angst*. To support her position that these verses describe an existence characterized by "the inability of the person to plan or carry out purposeful action," and that "what is lost is not simply the capacity to act but the meaningfulness of action," Newsom references Philippe Nemo and describes his book as one that understands Job's situation through the concept of Heideggerian *Angst*.[44]

For Job, both the pleasure of human contact and the exercise of power are found to be sources of frustration. As an example of the pleasure of human contact (the will to pleasure), we read in 3:7, "O, let that night be barren; let no joyful cry come in it." Newsom describes the verse as "a barren night, when no child is conceived, when there is no cry of sexual pleasure."[45] Other fundamental examples of human contact include Job's grief that his mother's lap and breasts were able to receive him, such that he did not die shortly after birth.[46] As an example of the will to power, we find the kings and counselors of the earth described in 3:14b as those "who are building

---

42. Frankl, *The Will to Meaning*, 84; Frankl, *The Feeling of Meaninglessness*, 61.
43. Frankl, *The Will to Meaning*, 59, 83.
44. Newsom, *The Book of Job*, 96. See also Nemo, *Job and the Excess of Evil*, in which Job and Heidegger are discussed.
45. Newsom, *The Book of Job*, 94.
46. Newsom, *The Book of Job*, 95.

ruins for themselves." Newsom comments that the section describes "the turmoil of existence . . . that derives from the exercise of power."[47]

We cannot help but notice the similarity of material found in chapter 3 and Frankl's historic placement of logotherapy. Like Job in chapter 3, Frankl sees the will to pleasure and the will to power as inferior expressions. He calls both "mere derivatives of man's primary concern, that is, the will to meaning."[48] For logotherapy, the will to meaning, or the basic desire of the human person to find and fulfill meaning, completes the sequence. With Job, however, the sequence in chapter 3 ends without the will to meaning. Job is left in turmoil.

Both Boss and Cox provide further support for our notion that chapter 3 represents the existential vacuum. Because Job has successfully passed the tests of the prologue, Boss asserts that chapter 3 is the beginning of an existential discussion, though Boss understands the meaning of that discussion somewhat differently than does logotherapy. Boss reflects that Job sees the totality of his life as having been ruined and wishes to have never been born.[49] In essence, Boss states the inverse of logotherapy's position when he says, "The need for life's meaning must be the need for the meaning of life as a whole. If life has at one time meaning, and then none, the loss of meaning must be the loss of meaning for life before the loss as well as after."[50] Although both Boss and Frankl would agree that life as a whole either has meaning or it does not, logotherapy asserts that meaning can never be taken away from a life once it is realized.[51]

Therefore, we must pause and consider what Job is lacking. What is missing that makes for a vacuum? As we have seen, Job has exercised the attitudinal value, a significant source of meaning in logotherapy. Specifically, he has held on to his integrity, rejected nihilism and reductionism, and has refused to curse God. As we have seen in 1:21, Job says, "Yahweh has given and Yahweh has seized; the Name of Yahweh be blessed." He continues this attitudinal value in 2:10 where he says, "We have been receiving good from Elohim, but shall we not receive evil?" He has retained his humanity despite suffering; this is something logotherapy insists is a human achievement. Frankl writes, "Once an individual's search for meaning has been successful,

---

47. Newsom, *The Book of Job*, 95.
48. Frankl, *The Will to Meaning*, 35.
49. Boss, *Human Consciousness of God*, 35–36, 38.
50. Boss, *Human Consciousness of God*, 41.
51. Frankl, *The Feeling of Meaninglessness*, 100; Frankl, *Man's Search for Meaning*, 150.

it renders him not only happy but also gives him the capability to cope with suffering."[52] Concerning the attitudinal value in particular, Frankl says that "even the helpless victim of a hopeless situation, facing a fate he cannot change, may rise above himself, may grow beyond himself, and by doing so change himself. He may turn a personal tragedy into a triumph."[53] Yet Job wishes he was never born.

The key to understanding this inconsistency can be found, our hermeneutic suggests, in the frustration Job expresses with human contact and with the exercise of power. No expression of the value of his attitude can be found in chapter 3 despite the fact that his characteristic wholeness and integrity are accorded great value in the prologue. For this reason, according to a logotherapy reading, what might otherwise be an occasion to recognize the experiential value (his mother lovingly receiving a newborn infant), or an occasion to recognize the creative value (kings and counselors engaged in the act of building), becomes nothing more than inferior expressions of a frustrated will to meaning.

Moreover, Job expands the scope of the existential vacuum and curses not only his own birth, but the birth of creation itself. He curses his day in terms of day and night, light and darkness. Habel's translation of 3:4–6 is particularly stunning: "That day! Let it be darkness! Let Eloah above not seek it! Let no light shine on it! Let darkness and death's shadow reclaim it! Let cloud hang over it! Let demons of the day terrify it! That night! Let sinister dark take it! Let it not be counted in the days of the year! Let it not appear in any of the months!"[54] Job essentially is wishing that the light be deprived and the darkness prolonged to eternity. In other words, Job is wishing for the reversal of creation wherein light is never called into being, order is never brought out of chaos. Verses 7–10 elaborate on this idea by associating the night with the womb. Just as Job wishes for light to never have come to the night, so he wishes for fertility to never have come to the womb.[55]

This idea is further developed in 3:8, translated by Habel as: "Let it be damned by those who curse day! By those ready to rouse Leviathan!"[56] Our hermeneutic (informed at this point by historical-criticism) understands

52. Frankl, *Man's Search for Meaning*, 139.
53. Frankl, *Man's Search for Meaning*, 146.
54. Habel, *The Book of Job*, 98–99.
55. Cox, *The Triumph of Impotence*, 40–42.
56. Habel, *The Book of Job*, 99.

Leviathan as a symbol of the primordial chaos out of which God created the world. Habel notes that reference to Leviathan as a violent sea monster is found in Canaanite mythology; Baal battles it. Yahweh also overcomes Leviathan in Isaiah 27:1 and Psalm 74:13–14 where Yahweh is said to crush its heads.[57] (Leviathan is depicted as a serpent-dragon with seven heads in an Akkadian cylinder seal).[58] Cox points out that Psalm 74 sees crushing Leviathan as one of the first works of God in the establishment of night and day. While Cox acknowledges that many authors see Job as calling on professional magicians and astrologers in 3:8, he believes that such professionals, though they may offer a formal curse, would not be properly described as "skilled in rousing Leviathan." He asserts that "rousing Leviathan" is much more than a wish to have never been born. "Those who are prepared to do it are reckless beyond measure," he writes, for "rousing Leviathan" is an undoing of the work of creation itself.[59]

These images of creation, and of Leviathan in particular, are understood by our logotherapy hermeneutic to be symbolic of ultimate meaning. Ultimate meaning is meaning that cannot be known; it is beyond the capacity of the human person to understand. Frankl calls it "a world beyond man's world."[60] Certainly, Leviathan is beyond the human world! According to logotherapy, this "world beyond" is also the only world in which the meaning of human suffering can be found. This means, as Frankl writes, "Man is incapable of understanding the *ultimate* meaning of human suffering."[61] By expanding the scope of his existential turmoil to include the cosmic dimension, our hermeneutic finds that Job is wedding his sense of meaning to something about which he can have no knowledge, namely, ultimate meaning. This makes Job's existential vacuum inevitable. For logotherapy, the solution is to separate ultimate meaning from the meaning of the moment—that is, meaning that can be realized through *experiencing, doing,* and *choosing*. It remains to be seen if Job discovers a similar solution.

57. Habel, *The Book of Job*, 108.
58. Gaster, "Leviathan," 116.
59. Cox, *The Triumph of Impotence*, 42.
60. Frankl, *The Will to Meaning*, 145.
61. Frankl, *The Will to Meaning*, 145; italics added.

THE DIALOGUE (JOB 4:1—27:23): THE LOGOTHERAPY OF JOB AND HIS FRIENDS

At the end of chapter 2, Job's three friends "made an appointment together to come to console him and to comfort him" (2:11b). Having sat with him in silence for seven days and seven nights, and now having heard his curse and the depth of his existential turmoil, the friends begin a dialogue with Job. Twice, Eliphaz, Bildad, and Zophar each speak in turn and are answered by Job. The third cycle of speeches is truncated and consists of an exchange between Eliphaz and Job followed by a brief statement by Bildad. Job then begins a soliloquy that is treated as a new section. Thus, there are seven complete exchanges: three with Eliphaz and two each with Bildad and Zophar.

The belief that existential turmoil can be overcome is fundamental to logotherapy. Frankl writes, "Man transcends himself either toward another human being or toward meaning."[62] Indeed, it is this capacity to reach toward meaning that is the opposite of Frankl's concept of the existential vacuum, or the feeling of meaninglessness. For Frankl, this is one of two basic capacities of the human spirit (the other being self-distancing). For the friends of Job, suffering is an expected part of life. "For humanity is born to trouble, [as] sparks fly upward" (5:6). Yet, this trouble can be overcome. "See, El will not reject the [one of] integrity nor strengthen the hand of evil ones. He will yet fill your mouth with laughter and your lips with shouting" (8:20–21). Both Frankl and the friends of Job are saying that suffering can be transcended, the former by the discovery of meaning and the latter by integrity.

As will be seen, the friends give Job specific suggestions. It is likely that Job himself was already well acquainted with their recommendations. In 4:3 the friends remind Job, "Look, you have instructed many and you have strengthened weak hands." Whatever social role the friends fulfill, it appears that their "consoling and comforting" is related in some way to "instructing and strengthening." In other words, they have something of the role of a logotherapist. Job may well be one of their number and now he is on the receiving end of the instruction.

Although logotherapy is recognized as one of the few existential-phenomenological approaches to develop specific techniques, it has always had an ambivalent relationship to technique. Frankl notes that logotherapy

---

62. Frankl, *The Will to Meaning*, 18–19.

is unique among existential psychologies because "it is possible to draw a proper technique out of it."⁶³ However, he explains elsewhere, "What matters is never technique per se but rather the spirit in which the technique is used. This holds not only for drugs and electroshocks, but for Freudian psychoanalysis, for Adlerian psychology, and for logotherapy as well."⁶⁴ As a phenomenological theory, Frankl states, "Phenomenology is an attempt to describe the way in which man understands himself, in which he interprets his own existence, far from preconceived patterns of interpretation and explanation." Continuing, he says that psychotherapy "goes beyond pure science in that it is wisdom. But even wisdom is not the last word. . . . Wisdom is lacking without the human touch."⁶⁵

This means that logotherapy would not offer Job a meaning for his suffering. Logotherapy only says that Job must discover his own meaning for his life as he experiences it. Frankl explains, "I have said that meaning cannot be arbitrarily given but must be found responsibly."⁶⁶ Furthermore, "Since this meaning is something unique, it does not fall under a general law. . . . Time and again, an individual's conscience commands him to do something which contradicts what is preached by the society."⁶⁷

Newsom provides support for our idea that the friends attempt something resembling therapy. She goes so far as to refer to the "therapeutic practices" of the friends, but, in distinction to logotherapy, explains that they offer Job a meaning through which to understand his suffering, a meaning that corresponds to the wisdom of the culture.⁶⁸ She writes, "What Eliphaz, Bildad, and Zophar offer to their friend Job is no illusion, no irrelevant and insensitive advice that overlooks his 'true' situation. They offer him not simply solace but access to power, the opportunity to take action to influence his situation. They offer him a way beyond turmoil."⁶⁹ Stated differently, they offer him something of an anti-logotherapy: a dialogue that seeks to give Job meaning through cultural wisdom versus a dialogue that encourages Job to discover his own unique meaning.

---

63. Frankl, *On the Theory and Therapy*, 191.
64. Frankl, *The Will to Meaning*, 28–29.
65. Frankl, *The Will to Meaning*, 7–8.
66. Frankl, *The Will to Meaning*, 63.
67. Frankl, *The Will to Meaning*, 63.
68. Newsom, *The Book of Job*, 116.
69. Newsom, *The Book of Job*, 115.

With this important difference in mind, our logotherapy hermeneutic now takes up some examples of how logotherapy views the advice of the friends. These examples include references to the creative and experiential values, hope for the future based on the attitudinal value, openness toward the future based on a sound philosophy of life, and an understanding of ultimate meaning.

Logotherapy and the Friends of Job

Eliphaz begins the dialogue by recalling Job's creative and experiential values. As we have seen, these are the values with which Job expresses frustration in chapter 3. Job had previously indicated that counselors were "building ruins for themselves" (3:14b). In 3:12a, Job asks, "Why did knees receive me?" Eliphaz, in contrast, affirms the value of creative and experiential values: "See, you have instructed many and have strengthened weak hands. Your words have upheld him who was stumbling and you have made firm tottering knees" (4:3–4). Logotherapy would do the same. In one of Frankl's most famous case studies, he demonstrates to a despondent and dying patient that the creative and experiential values actualized by her during the course of her life do not become meaningless with her death. Rather, they serve as a monument to her life. Following a therapy session in which he challenged her on the lasting value she had realized in her life, the last week of her life was described by hospital staff as being "full of faith and pride" rather than, as it was before the session, "agonized . . . ridden by the anxiety that she was useless."[70]

In chapter 3, Job had found the creative and experiential values meaningless and did not include any indication of an attitudinal value. We have suggested this lack of recognition of the attitudinal value is what is missing, responsible for the vacuum. Eliphaz attempts to restore it. First, he tries to help Job become critical of his attitude of impatience and dismay: "But now it has come to you and you are impatient. It touches you and you are dismayed" (4:5). He then recalls Job's former attitudinal value: "Is not your fear [of God] your confidence, and the integrity of your ways your hope?" (4:5). Frankl sees the attitudinal value as being the one most connected with the inevitability of suffering. He writes, "Attitudinal values . . . are actualized whenever the individual is faced with something unalterable, something

---

70. Frankl, *The Will to Meaning*, 123. The therapy transcript can be found on pages 120–23.

imposed by destiny. From the manner in which a person takes these things upon himself . . . there flows an incalculable multitude of value-potentialities. This means that *human life can be fulfilled not only in creating and enjoying, but also in suffering!*"[71] From the logotherapy perspective, if Job could see meaning in his fear of God and in his integrity, *for their own sake*, then retaining them despite his suffering would infuse his suffering with meaning. It would also answer the satan's challenge and demonstrate the authenticity of disinterested piety.

Eliphaz views suffering as inevitable, as we have seen. "For humanity is born to trouble, [as] sparks fly upward" (5:6). Nevertheless, Eliphaz sees suffering as a moment in time. The future may contain restoration. "For he wounds that he may bind; he wounds [severely] and his hands may heal" (5:18). Job, even, has the power to bring this future about based on choices he makes: "But I would seek El; and to Elohim I would commit my cause" (5:8). By placing Job's suffering in a context of inevitability, and yet potentially limited in time depending upon Job's choices, Eliphaz imagines a future open to change based on Job's own freedom of choice.

Frankl writes, "We must not overlook the fact that there are also tragic experiences inherent in human life . . . represented by the primordial facts of man's existence: suffering, guilt, and transitoriness."[72] No human life avoids these experiences. Nevertheless, the human person retains freedom of choice. In answering a question posed to him about the determinants of human behavior, Frankl answered "that as a neurologist and psychiatrist, of course, I am fully aware of the extent to which man is not at all free from conditions, be they biological, psychological, or sociological."[73] He continues, however, "that along with being a professor in two fields (neurology and psychiatry) I am a survivor of four camps (that is, concentration camps), and as such I also bear witness to the unexpected extent to which man is, and always remains, capable of resisting and braving even the worst conditions."[74] The central point that Frankl makes is that the human person remains open to the future just as Eliphaz implies. Concerning the nature of the human person, Frankl writes, "He, too, is sometimes portrayed as if he were merely a closed system within which cause-effect relations are oper-

---

71. Frankl, *The Doctor and the Soul*, 105–6; italics original.

72. Frankl, *The Feeling of Meaninglessness*, 189. This is the tragic triad, more commonly expressed by Frankl as pain, guilt, and death.

73. Frankl, *The Will to Meaning*, 16.

74. Frankl, *The Will to Meaning*, 16.

ant such as conditioned or unconditioned reflexes, conditioning processes or responses to stimuli."[75] Indeed, logotherapy views the human person as having been portrayed in exactly this way by the satan in 1:9–11. "On the other hand," Frankl continues, "being human is profoundly characterized as being open to the world."[76]

Newsom provides additional support for our position. In line with our recognition of Eliphaz's attempt to make Job aware of creative, experiential, and attitudinal values, Newsom writes, "If Job can make that connection, his sense of turmoil can be contained as he grasps his situation in relation to a story that includes images of purposeful action and supportive relationships. This recognition would not make his pain less, but it would restore to him an essential part of his humanity."[77] She continues, "By placing Job's present moment of crisis in the middle of an yet uncompleted story, Eliphaz treats it as something that can be integrated and endowed with meaning, a direct response to Job's experience of it as simply and irreducibly 'turmoil.'"[78]

Newsom argues that stories that look to the past for explanation remain closed, just as Frankl views psychoanalysis and behavioral psychology. It is as if finding reasons for distress in the present makes it the inevitable result of the past. By looking to the future, however, Eliphaz keeps the story open. Newsom writes of Eliphaz's speech, "It opens up the space of a possible future, one that finds its logic in the agency of God, understood as fundamentally moral."[79] The focus is on the future and what Job may yet do. "They are thus not stories of explanation, which would move backward in time," Newsom explains, rather they tell of "a possible future . . . these are narratives of hope."[80]

Likewise, Frankl views logotherapy as moving beyond the focus on the past characteristic of Freudian psychoanalysis and, instead, focusing on goals yet to be achieved. He writes, "Psychotherapy was born when the attempt was first made to look behind physical symptoms for their psychic causes . . . Now, however, a further step must be taken."[81] The position of logotherapy is that meanings actualized remain forever. Once actualized,

---

75. Frankl, *The Feeling of Meaninglessness*, 159.
76. Frankl, *The Feeling of Meaninglessness*, 159.
77. Newsom, *The Book of Job*, 101.
78. Newsom, *The Book of Job*, 102.
79. Newsom, *The Book of Job*, 103.
80. Newsom, *The Book of Job*, 103.
81. Frankl, *The Doctor and the Soul*, 11.

"they are rendered realities at that very moment."[82] By making a choice in the present, the future remains open. "At any moment, man must decide, for better or worse, what will be the monument of his existence."[83]

Logotherapy holds that being aware of one's philosophical assumptions is central to maintaining meaning. Frankl states, "There is no psychotherapy without a theory of man and a philosophy of life underlying it. Wittingly or unwittingly, psychotherapy is based on them."[84] He later continues, "One would assume that we have to espouse a sound philosophy of life in order to show that life really does hold a meaning."[85] In other words, the adoption of a sound life philosophy is, for Frankl, the solution to the existential vacuum.[86] The friends of Job remind him of their assumptions about life.

Bildad demonstrates what we might call a philosophy of life through his allegory of the two plants. Habel's translation is particularly clear. Concerning the fate of the godless, Habel translates 8:12–13:

> One plant is still fresh and uncut
> When it withers, quicker than grass.
> Such are the paths of all who forget El;
> The hope of the godless will perish.[87]

In contrast, the blameless are described in 8:16–20:

> Another plant stays fresh, even in the sun;
> Its shoots reach beyond its garden;
> Over a rock pile its roots wind;
> A house of stone it spies.
> If its place should swallow it
> And deny, saying 'I did not see you,'
> Such is the joy of its way
> That from the dust it shoots up elsewhere.
> Truly El does not spurn the blameless,
> Nor does he hold the hand of evildoers.[88]

---

82. Frankl, *Man's Search for Meaning*, 120.
83. Frankl, *Man's Search for Meaning*, 121.
84. Frankl, *The Will to Meaning*, 15.
85. Frankl, *The Will to Meaning*, 84.
86. Frankl, *The Will to Meaning*, 84.
87. Habel, *The Book of Job*, 168.
88. Habel, *The Book of Job*, 168. See Habel, *The Book of Job*, 168–69 for a discussion of the challenging aspects of this translation. In particular, Habel argues that משוש should

Bildad's argument is that wickedness brings about its own end. Concerning the wicked, Bildad says, "His own schemes throw him down for he is cast into a net by his own feet" (18:7b–8a). Newsom explains that Bildad's position is "one of the most widespread and fundamental beliefs in the ancient Near East."[89] That is, the nature of the world is not dualistic, with equally opposed forces of good and evil, but rather, in Newsom's words, "The destruction of evil is self-generated."[90] The practical outcome of this belief is that it allows a person to be resilient in the face of evil and to be confident in opposing evil. Contrary examples, such as Job will later supply, can be easily dismissed as exceptions to the rule.[91]

In addition to reminding Job of what logotherapy calls the categorical values—ways in which meaning can be discovered through creating, experiencing, and choosing—and in addition to reminding Job of what the friends consider to be a sound philosophy of life, the friends also point Job toward another logotherapy concept that Job expresses in chapter 3: ultimate meaning. Earlier we proposed that Job is experiencing existential vacuum because he has tied the meaning of his life to an ultimate meaning about which he can have no knowledge and in the process has rejected meaning offered by the categorical values. As we have mentioned, logotherapy recognizes a sharp division between ultimate meaning and the meaning of the moment based on the categorical values.

Like logotherapy, Zophar also speaks of two "meanings." In 11:5–6a, Zophar says, "But, O, if only Elohim would speak and that he would open his lips to you and that he would tell you the secrets of wisdom. For there are two sides to [abiding] wisdom." Normally כפלים means "double," but Marvin Pope "translates 'two sides,' implying a hidden and a manifest side."[92] Zophar implies the manifest side of wisdom in 11:13–14. As Habel translates it, this kind of wisdom means to "order your mind and stretch out your hands toward him," and to "remove the iniquity in your hand and

---

be translated "joy" even though others believe the word makes no sense in this context. Habel understands the use of "joy" as ironic in that the plant has joy that the earth swallows it. However, the joy of the robust plant in its growth may also prefigure the passion with which the wild animals in the God speeches are said to engage in their various behaviors.

89. Newsom, *The Book of Job*, 121.

90. Newsom, *The Book of Job*, 120.

91. Newsom, *The Book of Job*, 121–22.

92. Pope, *Job*, 84–85. For further discussion of Pope's translation, see Habel, *The Book of Job*, 203.

let no deceit dwell in your tent."[93] Before this, however, Zophar explains that (hidden) wisdom is unknowable: "Can you find the depth of Eloah, or unto the end of Shaddai can you find? [It is] high[er] [than] heaven—what can you do? [It is] deep[er] than Sheol—what can you know?" (11:7–8). For logotherapy, the manifest and hidden sides to wisdom correspond to the meaning of the moment and ultimate meaning. The meaning of the moment is expressed through the categorical values of creating, experiencing, and choosing—elements reflected in 11:13–14. Ultimate meaning remains hidden. Frankl writes, "This ultimate meaning necessarily exceeds and surpasses the finite capacities of man; in logotherapy, we speak in this context of a super-meaning. What is demanded of man is . . . to bear this incapacity to grasp its unconditional meaningfulness in rational terms."[94] The importance of these two sides to meaning will recur.

Logotherapy and Job

In the end, however, we know that the friends fail in their attempt to comfort and console their friend. Job rejects their meaning, unmasks a weakness in their argument, and moves in his own, unique direction in the discovery of meaning. "Times of crisis . . . are often the occasions for the rejection of prior narratives and the embrace or construction of new ones," writes Newsom.[95] In the following sections, we will look through the lens of logotherapy at some of the elements of Job's movement toward meaning. Elements involved in Job's discovery of meaning include rejecting the philosophy of life of the friends, challenging the representation of time, unmasking the sadomasochistic elements of religion, and beginning to realize the creative, experiential, and attitudinal values in concrete, if unique, terms. Each of these elements is set in further dialogue with logotherapy.

Job challenges the assumptions of the friends that those of integrity prosper and that the wicked are punished. He expresses the sentiments of the wicked in 21:15: "What is Shaddai that we should serve him? And what profit do we get if we pray to him?" According to Job, the wicked live in safety, prosper with their herds, have happy children, sing and rejoice, and

---

93. Habel, *The Book of Job*, 202.

94. Frankl, *Man's Search for Meaning*, 118. "Super-meaning" is a term Frankl sometimes uses in place of "ultimate meaning." The latter occurs in his writings much more frequently than the former.

95. Newsom, *The Book of Job*, 101.

finally die in peace (21:9–13).⁹⁶ Newsom argues that Job presents a "mirror image" of the moral foundation of the world.⁹⁷ Turmoil (chaos, evil) is the true reality that underlies the world. The result of this position is dramatic and stark. As Newsom puts it, "The foundation that makes it meaningful to distinguish between the goodness of protecting the orphan and the abhorrence of denying food to the hungry is swept away."⁹⁸ It also sweeps away the meaning offered by the friends.

Logotherapy agrees that meaning need not be discovered in the assumptions of a society or in the philosophy of a culture. "Time and again," Frankl writes, "an individual's conscience commands him to do something which contradicts what is preached by the society to which the individual belongs."⁹⁹ Perhaps, at first, only one or a few individuals discover meaning in a creative, experiential, or attitudinal value different from that of the culture at large. However, once the meaningfulness of the new value is demonstrated, others may begin to find meaning in it as well. "The unique meaning of today is the universal value of tomorrow. This is the way religions are created and values evolve," he writes.¹⁰⁰

Job specifically challenges the representation of time. The friends view time as open—as a stage, so to speak, upon which new possibilities may be enacted. Job, in contrast, views time as closed. He describes it as "forced labor" (7:1b) that is ended by death. Job 7:6 reads, "My days are swifter than a loom and come to an end without hope." Again, in 7:16 we find, "I despise (life). I would not live forever. Let me alone for my days are a breath." It is this very same time horizon that Frankl sees as a reminder to find the meaning of the moment. He writes, "The meaning of human existence is based upon its irreversible quality."¹⁰¹ Frankl explains that if the human person lived forever, there would be nothing immoral about postponing responsibilities indefinitely. Tomorrow would always come. However, the knowledge of death is what makes a human person a morally responsible agent. Time becomes meaningful because the human person must make a choice as to what to do with it. Logotherapy, therefore, understands Job's statements about time to be a necessary step in his discovery of meaning.

96. Boss, *Human Consciousness of God*, 113–14.
97. Newsom, *The Book of Job*, 124.
98. Newsom, *The Book of Job*, 125.
99. Frankl, *The Will to Meaning*, 63.
100. Frankl, *The Will to Meaning*, 63.
101. Frankl, *The Doctor and the Soul*, 64.

Job also raises to consciousness the presence of sadomasochism in the advice of his friends.[102] We have already seen the statement of Eliphaz in 5:18: "For he wounds that he may bind; he wounds [severely] and his hands may heal." The friends, therefore, are advising Job to turn to God—the one who has wounded him severely—to be restored. The ability to unmask what was previously unconscious is one possible outcome of suffering according to logotherapy, provided that the suffering is unavoidable. Frankl writes, "As long as we are still suffering from a condition that ought not to be, we remain in a state of tension between what actually is on the one hand and what ought to be on the other hand. And only while in this state of tension can we continue to envision the ideal."[103] Put otherwise, Frankl means that suffering shows us the deficits of our current situation so that we can imagine a better one. He continues, "Suffering therefore establishes a fruitful, one might say a revolutionary, tension in that it makes for emotional awareness of what ought not to be."[104] It is this state of tension that allows Job to unmask what ought not to be in the arguments of the friends, and to discover his own meaning of the moment.

Inviting God to heal him invites God to view his body as an object, an object that God has already invaded and broken. Job sees himself as a target (7:20), a lion that is hunted (10:16), and someone at whom the enemy "looks daggers" (16:9). Newsom translates 16:12–14a in this way: "I was at ease, and he broke me in pieces; he seized me by the neck and shattered me; he set me up as his target; his archers surrounded me. He slashed open my kidneys, without mercy; he poured out my gall on the ground. He breached me, breach upon breach."[105] The masochism of turning to the abuser for help is matched by divine sadism. Job 9:30–31 says, "If I wash myself with snow and clean my hands with lye, you will yet plunge me into the pit and my garments will abhor me." Newsom sees reflected here "a divine loathing incensed at the appearance of righteousness or cleanness in the human." She further says, "This is a violence calculated to destroy the humanity of the one who is subject to it."[106]

The psychological purpose of this masochism is to avoid responsibility for one's own life. According to Newsom, "By embracing the

---

102. Newsom treats this topic at length in *The Book of Job*, 138–50.
103. Frankl, *The Doctor and the Soul*, 107–8.
104. Frankl, *The Doctor and the Soul*, 108.
105. Newsom, *The Book of Job*, 138.
106. Newsom, *The Book of Job*, 144.

masochistic perspective of human corruptibility (in both the physical and moral senses), one can locate being and meaning in God, that is, safely beyond the reach of all powers of destruction and meaninglessness."[107] She notes that in Mesopotamian literature "humble submission is the only stance imaginable."[108] The consequence of this view "is precisely the relief from the burden of individual existence, always vulnerable to ambiguity, anguish, loneliness, and meaninglessness. By positing the self as nothing and the object of surrender as absolute reality, the terrors of pain, death, and anomie can be transcended."[109]

Job takes this unconscious masochism, makes it conscious, and rejects it. In other words, he does not transfer meaning to God, as the friends suggest, because God is the very one responsible for his unjust suffering. In doing so, logotherapy would argue that Job takes the responsibility for the discovery of meaning upon himself. In the words of Frankl, "Man is responsible for what to do, whom to love, and how to suffer."[110] More specifically, he writes that "logotherapy has the task of bringing persons to consciousness of their responsibility; but beyond this it may not transmit to them concrete values of any sort."[111] He continues, "Acting out of this responsibility patients must push forward on their own to the concrete meaning of their personal existence."[112] So, by rejecting the masochism of submitting himself to an abusive God, Job becomes conscious of his own responsibility to find the meaning of his life; he becomes morally responsible.

Because Job can no longer tie his sense of meaning to an ultimate reality beyond his understanding, he must also begin to realize meaning in concrete terms. This is what Job had previously found to be a source of frustration. In other words, Job must find ways to actualize the creative, experiential, and attitudinal values that reflect this new realization of his own responsibility. Job begins to imagine realizing the creative value through the process of having a trial. In 19:25a, Job says, "For I know my redeemer lives." Much has been written about the גאל (redeemer) in Job. Most of the discussion centers on the question of whether the גאל is God or someone else. The identity of the גאל does not matter from the logotherapy point of

---

107. Newsom, *The Book of Job*, 143.
108. Newsom, *The Book of Job*, 141.
109. Newsom, *The Book of Job*, 143.
110. Frankl, *The Will to Meaning*, 74.
111. Frankl, *On the Theory and Therapy*, 172.
112. Frankl, *On the Theory and Therapy*, 172.

view. The important point is that Job has thought about *doing* something through engaging in this imagery, even imagining that his case could be won against all odds. The passion that flows from "the defiant power of the human spirit," such as Job's statement that "I will see Eloah" (19:26) argues that he is emerging from his turmoil, that meaning is returning to his existential vacuum.[113] Newsom, too, reinforces our logotherapy understanding that this process makes the turmoil of Job "organized, interpreted, and made meaningful."[114]

In addition to realization of the creative value, further evidence of the return of meaning is found through the experiential value that includes compassion for others among its expressions. In 24:12, Job says, "From out of the city, men groan and the soul of the fatally wounded cries for help, yet God pays no attention to their prayer." Job moves from consideration of his personal suffering to the suffering of humanity in general. "Being human," writes Frankl, "is directed to something other than itself."[115] What Frankl means is that meaning is found when one is able reach beyond the self and become concerned with others. Logotherapy sees Job's acknowledgement of the suffering of others as another step out of his turmoil. Boss agrees with this view and notes that Job's desire to find the meaning of his suffering involves a concern for the suffering of others.[116] Cox, too, notes that Job is no longer focused on his own personal suffering as was the case in chapter 3.[117]

Job 27:2–4 encompass Job's witness oath: "As El lives, who has taken away my right, and Shaddai, who has made my soul bitter, for as long as my breath is in me and the spirit of Elohim is in my nostrils, my lips will not speak falsehood and my tongue will not utter deceit." Frankl writes, "The noblest appreciation of meaning is reserved to those people who, deprived of the opportunity to find meaning in a deed, in a work, or in love, by the very attitude which they choose to this predicament, rise above it." He continues, "What matters is the stand they take—a stand which allows for transmuting their predicament into achievement, triumph, and heroism."[118]

---

113. Discussion of the defiant power of the human spirit, a common phrase in logotherapy, is found in Frankl, *Man's Search for Meaning*, 147.

114. Newsom, *The Book of Job*, 159.

115. Frankl, *The Will to Meaning*, 50.

116. Boss, *Human Consciousness of God*, 123–24.

117. Cox, *The Triumph of Impotence*, 67.

118. Frankl, *The Will to Meaning*, 70.

Job has now taken a stand. From the viewpoint of logotherapy, he has rediscovered the attitudinal value. He has emerged from the existential vacuum.

CONCLUSION

Job began with a life that logotherapy would see as full of realized meaning. Following the loss of meaning, Job is thrust into the existential vacuum, a state of turmoil, stripped of everything save the essence of his values—values of integrity and wholeness. His friends offer him meaning for his suffering by reminding him of meaning already found through the categorical values, by adopting a sound philosophy of life, and by recognizing the limits of human knowledge of the ultimate. However, as logotherapy asserts, meaning cannot be given. It must be discovered by the sufferer alone. By the end of the dialogue, Job has rejected the worldview offered by the friends and has begun to develop his own based on his unique experience of wholeness and integrity and his own experience of suffering. He then begins to imagine realizing creative and experiential values based on his own, new understanding. Finally, Job emerges from the existential vacuum as he once more learns to recognize the value of attitude, the value of his freedom to choose his response to his own suffering.

5

Job and Frankl's Will to Meaning

THE SECTION THAT WE now explore, chapters 28 to 37, begins and ends with wisdom poetry. In chapter 28 we explore the relationship between the poet's description of wisdom and Frankl's understanding of meaning. Job's monologue in chapters 29 to 31 are read as an existential self-analysis, that is, an analysis of personal meaning in the life of Job. The Elihu monologue of chapters 32 to 37 allow our logotherapy hermeneutic to explore issues of divine communication, the place of past suffering, and the exploration of meaning through the experiential value.

Meaning in logotherapy functions in the same way that wisdom does in the Book of Job. Both meaning and wisdom refer to the highest aspirations of the human person. For Frankl, this highest aspiration is "that which most deeply inspires man; . . . the innate desire to give as much meaning as possible to one's life, to actualize as many values as possible."[1] For Job, "Silver cannot be weighed as its price, nor can it be valued in the gold of Ophir" (28:15b–16a). It is something that is present and must be found. For Frankl, as we have seen, meaning must be discovered. For Job, wisdom must be sought. While both meaning and wisdom cannot be known in a certain sense, both, paradoxically, can be lived. Frankl makes this clear through the realization of his creative, experiential, and attitudinal values. As we will see, a similar realization of lived values concludes chapter 28.

James L. Crenshaw's definition of wisdom also contains striking parallels to Frankl's categorical values. He defines wisdom as "the quest for

---

1. Frankl, *The Doctor and the Soul*, xvi.

self-understanding in terms of relationships with things (nature wisdom), people (juridical and practical wisdom), and the Creator (theological wisdom)."[2] Habel says "wisdom is apparently the deep and mysterious principle behind all other laws, principles, and designs of the cosmos."[3] Paraphrasing logotherapy, we may even describe this section as demonstrating Job's will to wisdom.

THE WISDOM POEM (JOB 28:1–28): THE WILL TO MEANING

Many views exist among scholars regarding chapter 28. According to Habel, it is "a brilliant but embarrassing poem for many commentators. It has been viewed as an erratic intrusion, an inspired intermezzo, a superfluous prelude, and an orthodox afterthought."[4] Elsewhere he writes, "I now accept this poem as integral to the Book of Job and view it as a closure for the cycle of speeches between Job and his friends."[5] Hartley notes that the tone does not match that of any of the speakers in the dialogue with the friends. He states, "It functions as a bridge between the dialogue and the group of speeches that are coming."[6] Boss asserts that the text can be read in continuity with what comes before and after.[7] Cox ignores it. Newsom identifies chapter 28 as a new voice that has not yet been heard among the voices that have spoken so far.

Our logotherapy hermeneutic reads it according to Frankl's understanding of meaning. Although mention has been made of wisdom in the dialogue, the type of wisdom described by chapter 28 appears to be wisdom of a different nature. It is a transcendent wisdom not available to human understanding. This is illustrated well in 28:20–22: "From where does wisdom come and where is the place of understanding? For it is hid from the eyes of all the living and is concealed from the birds of the air. [Even] Abaddon and Death say, 'With our ears we have [only] heard a report of it.'" Wisdom in chapter 28 is something known only to God: "Elohim understands the way to it and knows its place" (28:23). The difference between the understanding

---

2. Crenshaw, "Method," 132.
3. Habel, "Wisdom in the Book of Job," 306.
4. Habel, *The Book of Job*, 391.
5. Habel, "Wisdom in the Book of Job," 305.
6. Hartley, *The Book of Job*, 373.
7. Boss, *Human Consciousness of God*, 138.

of transcendent wisdom in chapter 28 and Job's instrumental use of wisdom in the dialogue stands parallel to Frankl's understanding of ultimate meaning and the meaning of the moment. Specifically, there are parallels in the understanding that ultimate meaning is somehow a precondition to the meaningfulness of human life, in the ordering of values as a point of coherency, and in the lack of human ability to fully grasp the ultimate.

Meaning, for Frankl, is experienced subjectively by the human person, and yet remains an objective reality. The objectivity of the situation is what makes the subjective experience meaningful; otherwise, the experience would be no more meaningful than fantasy or hallucination. Frankl acknowledges that "to all appearances, meaning is just something we are projecting into the things around ourselves, things which in themselves are neutral."[8] He continues, however, asserting that "the only thing which is subjective is the perspective through which we approach reality, and this subjectiveness does not in the least detract from the objectiveness of reality itself."[9] He summarizes, "There is only one meaning to each situation, and this is its true meaning."[10]

This is a difficult concept for many contemporary thinkers. Frankl does not believe that reality is a social construct nor does he accept any type of moral relativism. For Frankl, there is one and only one correct, true meaning to be discovered in any situation. This meaning is partly, but not solely, a characteristic of the human person acting in the situation.[11] To give a greatly oversimplified example, suppose that a passerby came upon a woman having a heart attack. The meaning potential offered by the situation is to take action, the creative value, to save her life. The way in which this value is actualized would be different for different passersby. Those trained in medicine would have one response, whereas those not so trained would have another response. However, at no point does the situation offer a meaning in doing nothing, or in doing harm. The meanings of most actual moments in life are, of course, much more subtle, but no less objective for Frankl.

---

8. Frankl, *The Will to Meaning*, 59.
9. Frankl, *The Will to Meaning*, 59.
10. Frankl, *The Will to Meaning*, 61.
11. Frankl elaborates, "This is opposed to the contention of Jean-Paul Sartre that ideals and values are designed and invented by man. Or, as Jean-Paul Sartre has it, man invents himself." Frankl, *The Will to Meaning*, 60.

Job and Frankl's Will to Meaning

Frankl argues that for each unique combination of human person and situation, there exists one right meaning for the human person to realize, one right choice to make. Frankl does not mean that the human person will know for certain what this choice is, but the reality of the one right choice is a precondition for the human person to discover meaning, rather than to merely impose meaning. He writes, "Human beings are transcending themselves toward meanings which are something other than themselves, which are more than mere expressions of their selves, more than mere projections of these selves. Meanings are discovered but not invented."[12] The notion that meaning is objectively real in the world and not a function of human cognition is based on Frankl's phenomenology. Regarding the human person and objectivity, Frankl writes, "Unless his self-understanding is crippled by preconceived patterns of interpretation, not to say indoctrination, he refers to meaning as something to find rather than something to give."[13]

Our logotherapy hermeneutic reads 28:3 as reflective of this idea: "Men put an end to darkness and to every farthest limit. They search out ore in gloom and deep darkness." Wisdom, or meaning, is something to be sought. Nevertheless, it is not something that is clear and easily visible, rather it is something in deep darkness, something about which we cannot be certain. The one seeking meaning must acknowledge the limitations of the search. One would not search for ore in deep darkness unless one was convinced of the objective reality of the ore. Frankl writes, "If I am to search for meaning, I have to be certain that there is meaning. If, on the other hand, I cannot be certain that I will also find it, I must be tolerant."[14]

Frankl, also, speaks to the ordering of values.[15] While meanings are unique for Frankl, values are the result of similar meanings discovered in similar situations. He explains, "One may define values as those meaning universals which crystallize in the typical situations a society or even humanity has to face."[16] Moreover, while Frankl acknowledges that values may, at times, appear to be in conflict, this is a mistaken notion. He writes,

---

12. Frankl, *The Will to Meaning*, 60.
13. Frankl, *The Will to Meaning*, 61.
14. Frankl, *The Will to Meaning*, 66.
15. Frankl uses the word "values" here in a different way than he does when speaking of the "categorical values." The categorical values are means by which unique meaning can be discovered. Here, "value" refers to a cultural or societal norm in the sense of Scheler.
16. Frankl, *The Will to Meaning*, 56.

"The rank of a value is experienced together with the value itself. In other words, the experience of one value includes the experience that it ranks higher than another. There is no place for value conflicts."[17] Frankl means that values are not equivalent items such that one may correctly choose one over another by mere preference. Rather, a value contains within itself its own rank or position in relation to other values. Seen from this point of view, chapter 28 can be seen as a search for the value (or values) that both God and Job might appeal to as superordinate.

Newsom reads chapter 28 in a somewhat similar way. She notes that the meaningfulness of the moral order of the world exists only as a potential. In other words, it is possible that Job would be granted justice; the world would then make sense. However, in the wisdom poem the moral order of the world "exists as a deep structure not accessible to the rational consciousness, yet in some way is the essential precondition for meaningfulness in human life."[18] In addition, Newsom makes the point that this different view of wisdom also illuminates a previously unreferenced quest in Job's dialogue. "He is tunneling, overturning obstacles, sinking shafts in the search for something that is not only more precious than gold but beyond all other values," she writes.[19] He seeks "a point of coherency, a vantage point from which God, the world, and his own experience make sense. For Job, to be vindicated by God presumes the existence of a set of transcendent values, continuous between God and humankind, that serves as the ground by which the distortions of the world can be put right."[20] Job's mistake, as Newsom understands chapter 28, is in believing that human rationality can grasp this coherency.[21]

Logotherapy understands the position of chapter 28 to be that transcendent wisdom, this realization of coherency, is beyond human understanding. The transcendent wisdom of chapter 28 is something established by God: "Then [God] saw it and declared it. He established it and also explored it" (28:27). Frankl says of ultimate meaning: "This ultimate meaning necessarily exceeds and surpasses the finite intellectual capacities of man; in logotherapy, we speak in this context of a super-meaning."[22] He concludes,

17. Frankl, *The Will to Meaning*, 56–57.
18. Newsom, *The Book of Job*, 177.
19. Newsom, *The Book of Job*, 177.
20. Newsom, *The Book of Job*, 177.
21. Newsom, *The Book of Job*, 177.
22. Frankl, *Man's Search for Meaning*, 118.

"*Logos* is deeper than logic."²³ What Frankl asserts here is that meaning (*logos*) may be experienced in ways deeper than the purely intellectual.

This is not the final word, however. Another view of wisdom emerges, culminating in 28:28 that says, "And [God] said to the human, 'See, the fear of Adonai, that is wisdom and to turn from evil is understanding.'" We have commented earlier on the activistic nature of logotherapy. Again and again Frankl speaks of meaning in terms of action: *creating, experiencing, choosing*. Meaning is not something to be understood, but something to be lived. Frankl explains, "Logotherapy, keeping in mind the essential transitoriness of human existence, is not pessimistic but rather activistic."²⁴ He elaborates on this when he says, "I wish to stress that the true meaning of life is to be discovered in the world rather than with man or his own psyche."²⁵ That is to say, in view of the fact of suffering and death, logotherapy is about realizing meaning through purposeful activity. Such an activist, according to Frankl, "can reflect with pride and joy on all the richness . . . on all the life he has already lived to the fullest."²⁶ Speaking for the activist, Frankl writes, "I have realities in my past, not only the reality of work done and of love loved, but of sufferings bravely suffered. These sufferings are even the things of which I am most proud."²⁷ Thus, just as chapter 28 concludes with the discovery of wisdom through a way of living, so also, Frankl discovers meaning by living.

Although 28:28 is often regarded as a pious insertion, Newsom provides support for our position when she argues that this verse takes terms from the prologue and redefines them according to its own understanding. "See—the fear of the Lord—that is wisdom; and turning from evil—understanding."²⁸ She elaborates that the prose tale made no mention of wisdom and understanding; yet, for the poet of chapter 28, a deeper meaning can be discerned. What Newsom means here is that chapter 28 sees within the prologue a way of living that can be understood from the viewpoint of wisdom. The viewpoint of wisdom, she explains, is different from the viewpoint of a seeker. She writes, "Thus, one realizes that the poem is in no sense saying that humans have no access to wisdom. They will not

23. Frankl, *Man's Search for Meaning*, 118; italics original.
24. Frankl, *Man's Search for Meaning*, 121.
25. Frankl, *Man's Search for Meaning*, 110.
26. Frankl, *Man's Search for Meaning*, 121.
27. Frankl, *Man's Search for Meaning*, 122.
28. Newsom, *The Book of Job*, 181.

find it if they look for it as an object (even an intellectual object) but only if they also know it through a comparable mode of being, a way of acting."[29] According to Newsom, the wisdom poem asserts that life can be lived from within this viewpoint, from within the coherency of wisdom. She writes, "Such a way of living does not entitle one to expect freedom from trouble (contra Prov 3:21–26 and the like). The coherency and meaningfulness of such a life is to be found as much within suffering as within peace."[30]

It is in the *redefinition* of the "fear of the Lord" wherein wisdom (or meaning) may be discovered coherently.[31] Just as in our simplified example of a passerby trained in medicine and a passerby not so trained, so, too, would the concept of the "fear of the Lord" be a cultural given for some and not for others. However, the uniqueness of a given situation must be discovered by each. For the person who has been trained in the concept of the "fear of the Lord," as the poet of chapter 28 has, each unique situation offers the possibility of discovering what the "fear of the Lord" means in each unique, and objective, situation. For purposes of illustration, if we equate "fear of the Lord" with "obeying the commandments," then an actual example is given by Frankl in his final words to his first wife, as we referenced earlier. That is, respecting his marriage vows might be "fear of the Lord" in one circumstance, but releasing those vows (in the unrealized hope that his first wife might survive the concentration camp) might be "fear of the Lord" in another.[32] Thus, two opposite actions are held together in a coherent and meaningful way for Frankl.

Boss also makes some observations relevant to the logotherapy understanding. He notes a change in the question from where wisdom is found to from where wisdom comes. In the former, wisdom is seen as a passive object to be discovered. In the latter, wisdom is coming forth actively. He states, "The verses which follow are about living, active wisdom, which can be met only from life in its fullness, as 28:28 will conclude."[33] What Boss means is that wisdom can be realized through the actions of a human person even if a human person cannot understand wisdom itself. Boss points out that

---

29. Newsom, *The Book of Job*, 180.

30. Newsom, *The Book of Job*, 181.

31. Speculatively, one might suggest that this redefinition is signaled by the use of אדני in 28:28 rather than אלהים as used in 1:1.

32. For more background on this incident, see Frankl, *The Will to Meaning*, 63–64 and Fabry, *The Pursuit of Meaning*, 62.

33. Boss, *Human Consciousness of God*, 142.

Job was already described in the prologue as one who fears God and shuns evil. He suggests that what has changed for Job is an understanding of the difference between human wisdom, which he has, and divine wisdom, or wisdom itself, which remains a mystery.[34] As Boss states, "Wisdom . . . is not to be found by mere searching. It comes. Furthermore, wisdom is God's way with created things. Job glimpses wisdom. Then he realizes that it is for him to be open to it."[35] He writes, "From the human point of view, wisdom is to stand in awe of God and eschew evil. It is not to be pursued but lived."[36]

THE MONOLOGUE OF JOB (JOB 29:1—31:40): AN EXISTENTIAL SELF-ANALYSIS

To paraphrase logotherapy, chapters 29–31 comprise Job's personal will to wisdom. It is a monologue wherein Job reflects on his life: his past, his present, and the way in which he has chosen to live. In some ways, then, it shares affinity with what Frankl calls the special existential analysis, defined as his method of revealing consciousness of responsibility "with particular emphasis upon case histories."[37] In other words, it is an account of one person's own unique experience with meaning and responsibility for living. We will examine it through this lens. Other commentators hold a variety of viewpoints. Cox, for example, views this section as a lament and even calls it "a classic example of the genre."[38] Boss sees it as standing in opposition to chapter 3.[39] (If so, then our hermeneutic would expect these chapters to also stand in opposition to Job's existential turmoil, that is to say, to stand in solidarity with the apprehension of meaning). Newsom states that it "does not appear to be cast as a recognizable genre."[40] She asserts that the consensus view is that it does not follow a particular literary form, but rather eclectically combines numerous models. She conceptualizes it as a testimony defined as "the giving of an account of events, of one's experience, or of oneself."[41]

34. Boss, *Human Consciousness of God*, 143.
35. Boss, *Human Consciousness of God*, 145.
36. Boss, *Human Consciousness of God*, 159.
37. Frankl, *The Doctor and the Soul*, 176.
38. Cox, *The Triumph of Impotence*, 102.
39. Boss, *Human Consciousness of God*, 146.
40. Newsom, *The Book of Job*, 184.
41. Newsom, *The Book of Job*, 185.

Viewed from the logotherapy standpoint, this section makes a smooth transition from the wisdom poem. The wisdom poem ended with the notion that wisdom could be discovered by action. In the monologue, Job is taking action through his speech. "O that there was one to hear me," Job says in 31:35. "Here is my signature; let Shaddai answer me," Job continues after having presented examples of the life he has lived. In light of the wisdom poem, this could be seen as an attempt to realize wisdom. According to Cox, having refuted the arguments of the friends, the existential tradition leaves two alternatives open to Job: he can accept the way things are, or he can revolt against the way things are. According to Cox, "Job's reaction is one of revolt."[42] He continues, "This is Job's final gesture, a cry of 'no surrender!'"[43]

Logotherapy resonates with this defiance. Frankl does not define what he calls "the defiant power of the human spirit," but rather illustrates it with the story of Jerry Long. As an athletic young man, the future Dr. Long had a promising career in major league baseball before a diving accident left him paralyzed from the neck down. Having lost his physical abilities, he focused on his mental abilities, becoming a clinical psychologist and expert in logotherapy. Frankl quotes a letter he received from him: "I view my life as being abundant with meaning and purpose. The attitude that I adopted on that fateful day has become my personal credo for life: I broke my neck, it didn't break me."[44] Frankl elaborates his point: "Is this to say that suffering is indispensable to the discovery of meaning? In no way. I only insist that meaning is available in spite of—nay, even through—suffering, provided . . . that the suffering is unavoidable."[45] Cox sees the same in Job. He states, "We are left with a situation of revolt. The cry of a man lost in the sea of existence, devoid of map-readings or direction, and refusing to the last gasp to accept and conform to his situation."[46] We next turn to some examples.

Job reflects on his past as a time when "Elohim watched over me, when his lamp shone upon my head. I walked through darkness by his light" (29:2b–3). Job goes on to recount various acts of justice and charity as well as acts reflecting the honor he was given by those around him. The experiential value is recognized by Job in 29:5 where he reflects on a time

42. Cox, *The Triumph of Impotence*, 100.
43. Cox, *The Triumph of Impotence*, 100.
44. Frankl, *Man's Search for Meaning*, 147.
45. Frankl, *Man's Search for Meaning*, 147.
46. Cox, *The Triumph of Impotence*, 112.

"when Shaddai was with me; my children were around me." This value is reflected not only in the home, but also in the community: "Young men saw me and drew back and the aged rose and stood" (29:8). The creative value is recognized through Job's counsel: "[Others] listened to me and waited and kept silence for my counsel. After my word, they did not speak again, and upon them my word [gently] fell" (29:21–22). Job also recognizes the attitudinal value, something he was unable to do in chapter 3. This is reflected in 29:14 where Job says, "I put on integrity and it clothed me like a robe, and my justice a turban."

What becomes clear from Job's existential self-analysis, however, is that expectations were tied to the expression of these values. In 29:18 Job reveals, "Then I thought, 'I will die in my house and I shall multiply my days as the sand.'" Thus we might restate the satan's question: Does Job realize the categorical values for their own sake (the logotherapy equivalent of disinterested piety), or does he do so to earn these expectations (to be an automaton of the environment in Frankl's words)? Regardless of the answer, Job's expectations are far from realized. "I cry to you and you do not answer me" (30:20a). "I looked for good, but evil came and when I waited for light, then came darkness" (30:26).

In addition to Job's recollection of the categorical values, he also reflects upon the notion of responsibility. One example of this is his preservation of justice: "If I have rejected the judgment of my slave or my handmaid when they brought a suit against me, then what shall I do when El rises up and when he makes inquiry, what will I answer him?" (31:14). Responsibility is deeply intertwined with meaning in logotherapy. Frankl states that the human person "is responsible for using the passing opportunities to actualize potentialities, to realize values, whether creative, experiential, or attitudinal. In other words, man is responsible for what to do, whom to love, and how to suffer."[47] This sense of responsibility is expressed in the categorical imperative of logotherapy: "Live as if you were living already for the second time and as if you had acted the first time as wrongly as you are about to act now!"[48] Frankl laments, however, that society is not yet completely aware of its responsibility, unlike the claim made individually by Job. Frankl explains that if it were, then "we would realize that there is

---

47. Frankl, *The Will to Meaning*, 74.
48. Frankl, *Man's Search for Meaning*, 109.

plenty of meaning waiting to be fulfilled by us, be it with respect to underprivileged people or with respect to underdeveloped countries."[49]

Indeed, Job, too, seems to recognize meaning fulfillment in relation to his responsibility toward the powerless of his society. "Job's social identity, his very meaning, must be established in terms of his relationship with the poor and powerless," explains Newsom.[50] In other words, Job has acted responsibly with the power that came from being the embodiment of the highest values of his society. Though it would have been possible for him to pervert justice, he took care to maintain it. Boss explains that by repeated use of an oath of clearance—if I have done this, then let that happen—Job is accepting responsibility for any wrong he has done. Boss explains, "In doing this he sees right action as being within the context of social justice and of equality before God. He expresses the experience of a great and overwhelming awe of God, but is nevertheless fearless before God in defending the truth about himself."[51]

Job has now stated the meaningfulness of his life in terms of responsibly realizing the categorical values. His next realization is that the apparent meaninglessness of his suffering can be made meaningful retroactively. Bringing us back to Job's defiant spirit, he says in 31:35b–36, "Here is my signature; let Shaddai answer me; let my accuser answer me by written indictment. Surely I would carry it on my shoulder and bind it on myself as a crown." The implication is that if Job is granted justice from God, then meaning can be restored.

Our reading is influenced by our understanding of honor-based societies. Having identified himself with the highest values of his society, and having demonstrated his responsibility in the exercise of power based on those values, Job challenges his listeners (whomever they may be) to do the same. According to Newsom, Job "subtly shifts them into the position of judging between himself and God."[52] Moreover, he has done so diplomatically. His appeal is one that preserves "the honor of all parties rather than the honoring of one at the expense of the shaming of the other."[53] God, as depicted in Job's oaths of chapter 31 is, also, identified with the highest values of Job's society, as Job has already identified himself. According to

49. Frankl, *The Will to Meaning*, 98.
50. Newsom, *The Book of Job*, 189.
51. Boss, *Human Consciousness of God*, 157.
52. Newsom, *The Book of Job*, 193.
53. Newsom, *The Book of Job*, 195.

Newsom, "The brilliance of this rhetorical stance is that the God Job represents in his oath *could not but* declare Job to be righteous and so confirm his honor."[54] Newsom explains the dynamics of the argument further: "What God requires of Job is what Job expects of God. That it would not be a matter of shame is evident in the fact that Job himself uses this example as evidence of his own honorableness."[55] In other words, Job is inviting God to be the God of his expectations, or the God of his actualized values.

Although logotherapy asserts, as does Job, that meaning can be restored retroactively, the dynamic is different. Frankl writes, "When we are no longer able to change a situation . . . we are challenged to change ourselves."[56] Job is not advocating changing himself. Instead, he is advancing an argument to persuade his listeners (or God) to grant him justice. However, according to logotherapy, we discover meaning in the past by changing ourselves in the present. Just as the man Frankl calls "the mass murderer of Steinhof" was later described as having "lived up to the highest conceivable moral standard," so logotherapy asserts that anyone can transmute a flawed past into a meaningful one by choosing meaningful values in the present.[57] Frankl states this another way when he writes, "Man does not simply exist but always decides what his existence will be, what he will become in the next moment."[58]

Still, from the point of view of our logotherapy hermeneutic, Job has discovered his will to meaning. He has recognized the meaningful elements of his life prior to the onset of his suffering in terms of the creative, the experiential, and the attitudinal values. He has recognized the importance of responsibly living out these values. He acknowledges that his life can yet be meaningful. This is a significant change from the Job of chapter 3. However, meaning for Job is still based on something outside his control; it is still based on God hearing him and acknowledging the justice of his cause. For logotherapy, while meaning reaches toward someone or something else, it does not originate there. It is deeply personal; it can never be denied or taken away by others. It remains to be seen if Job will make this discovery as well.[59]

54. Newsom, *The Book of Job*, 196; italics original.
55. Newsom, *The Book of Job*, 197.
56. Frankl, *Man's Search for Meaning*, 112.
57. Frankl, *Man's Search for Meaning*, 132.
58. Frankl, *Man's Search for Meaning*, 131.
59. To borrow from the vocabulary of contemporary psychotherapy, Job has returned

THE MONOLOGUE OF ELIHU (JOB 32:1—37:24): ADDITIONAL TOPICS

It is well accepted that the intervention of Elihu is a later addition that disrupts the flow of the story. Cox ignores it, as he did chapter 28, treating Job's monologue as part of the dialogue. For our purposes, we may agree with Boss who writes, "The history of the text is not here of concern, and the speeches of Elihu will be taken as we find them, and where we find them."[60] Newsom demonstrates an openness to Elihu that appears rather unique among commentators. She explains that it is her desire "to view him with a more dispassionate and deliberately generous curiosity."[61] Despite Newsom's generosity, she still notes that the Elihu intrusion upsets the symmetry of the Book of Job and "serves to this day as an irritant."[62]

Of particular interest is that Newsom designates Elihu as a "reader." Up to this point, we have placed logotherapy into dialogue with the text based on the thoughts and associations to Frankl's material that a logotherapist, a contemporary reader of the text, would have. However, Elihu, a reader in a different place and time, has inserted his thoughts and associations into the text itself at the critical point between the end of the words of Job and the beginning of the speeches of God. Consequently, the Elihu speeches may be seen as the first commentary on the Book of Job. Placing logotherapy into dialogue with it may be of some interest, as one reader to another.

From the point of view of logotherapy, Elihu raises three relevant points for discussion. These include the nature of divine communication, the value of suffering, and further discussion on the nature of wisdom that we identify with logotherapy's understanding of meaning. This latter discussion makes use of Newsom's identification of a wisdom genre she refers to as the sapiential nature hymn.[63]

---

to his previous level of functioning; he is roughly as aware of himself as he was in the prologue. In the context of psychotherapy practice, logotherapy (like other forms of therapy) seeks to return a patient to the level of functioning prior to the onset of the presenting problems. Unlike many other forms of therapy, however, logotherapy sees this as merely the first step. The next step is to allow the patient to develop an even higher level of functioning than she experienced before the onset of the problems. For further discussion of the psychological points raised, see Frankl, *Man's Search for Meaning*, 65–66; Frankl, *The Will to Meaning*, 50; Frankl, *On the Theory and Therapy*, 3–4.

60. Boss, *Human Consciousness of God*, 160.
61. Newsom, *The Book of Job*, 201.
62. Newsom, *The Book of Job*, 201.
63. Newsom, *The Book of Job*, 207, 211, 216, 220.

The Nature of Divine Communication

Elihu argues that Job's manner of approaching God is flawed. In 35:12–14 he says, "There they cry out, but he does not answer because of the pride of the wicked. Surely, El does not hear an empty cry nor does Shaddai regard it. How much less when you say that you do not see him, that the case is before him and you are waiting for him!" According to Elihu, God does speak. Job, however, has failed to hear his voice. Elihu says in Job 33:14, "For in one way, El speaks. And in two, though he does not see it." Or, less literally, "In one way or another, El speaks, though [humanity] does not perceive it." Elihu identifies dreams, pain, and angels (33:15, 19, 23) as means by which God communicates. Continuing in 33:15–16, Elihu explains, "In a dream, in a vision of night, when deep sleep falls upon men, while they sleep on beds, then he opens the ears of men and seals their warnings that he may turn a person from his deed and may hide pride from [the] defender."[64]

Somewhat surprisingly, logotherapy also takes up the issue of "divine" communication; noetic communication takes place through the human conscience. Frankl writes, "Conscience is fully understandable only against the background of a transhuman dimension."[65] Frankl argues that, like the human navel, the phenomenon of conscience can only be understood by reference to something other than the person herself. Moreover, this implies for Frankl that the human person has a responsibility toward someone or something else. We have discussed logotherapy's emphasis on responsibility before. For Frankl, this responsibility rests on the assumption that the human person is responsible to this transpersonal agent implied by conscience. He elaborates, "To explain man's being free, the existential quality of the human reality would do; however, to explain his being responsible, the transcendent quality of conscience must be considered."[66]

Frankl views the conscience as irreducible. It is not the same for Frankl as the super-ego is for Freud. He writes, "Conscience not only refers to transcendence; it also originates in transcendence . . . Therefore, if we raise the question of the origin of conscience, there can be no psychological answer

---

64. These verses use אנשים that I am translating "men" to indicate persons of male gender. The more generalized אדם is translated "person." The final term מגבר is used to separate a man particularly from those he is culturally obliged to defend, namely women and children. I am translating it with the word "defender."
65. Frankl, *Man's Search for Ultimate Meaning*, 61.
66. Frankl, *Man's Search for Ultimate Meaning*, 61.

but only an ontological one."⁶⁷ Therefore, in Frankl's thought, conscience is a uniquely human phenomenon that has its origin in transcendence. By extension, the nature of what it means to be a human person has its origin in transcendence. He writes, "The very term 'person,' seen in this light, takes on a new meaning, for now one may say: Through the conscience of the human person, a transpersonal agent *per-sonat*—which literally means, 'is sounding through.'"⁶⁸

Frankl speaks of the "sounding through," or the voice of conscience, as a means by which a transpersonal agent may be heard. However, both the logotherapist, as a contemporary reader, and Elihu, as an ancient reader, make reference to another means by which a spiritual or transcendent message may make itself heard: dreams. He explains, "Since Freud introduced the classical method of dream interpretation, based on free associations, we have learned to avail ourselves of this technique."⁶⁹ Frankl's purpose is different from Freud's, however. He explains, "Our goal is to lift not only instinctual but also spiritual phenomena into consciousness—and into responsibleness."⁷⁰

It may seem as if we have strayed somewhat far afield, but the discussion helps us position logotherapy with respect to Elihu in a somewhat linear way. The line drawn may be thought of as a movement from the concrete, to the mystical, to the transcendental. To begin with, Job desires for God to answer his petition in a concrete way. Elihu, a later reader, objects to this notion and asserts that God does, in fact, speak—through dreams, through pain, and through angels. It is merely the case that Job has not been listening. Logotherapy has moved in the same direction as Elihu, asserting that a transpersonal agent can make itself known through the voice of conscience, and that this voice may also influence dreams. This same linear pattern may also be seen in Elihu's next contribution.

The Place of Past Suffering

Elihu also says that divine communication may take place through pain. In 33:19a, he says, "He is proved with pain upon his bed." If we take והוכח to mean "is chastened," then logotherapy would disagree. However, if we

---

67. Frankl, *Man's Search for Ultimate Meaning*, 63.
68. Frankl, *Man's Search for Ultimate Meaning*, 60.
69. Frankl, *Man's Search for Ultimate Meaning*, 47.
70. Frankl, *Man's Search for Ultimate Meaning*, 47.

take the word to mean "is proved," then there is some possibility that Elihu could be referring to the capacity of the human person to discover meaning despite suffering. In this sense, the human person may prove to herself that life retains meaning despite suffering. As it happens, the word occurring in this verb form (Hoph'al) is a *hapax legomenon*. Boss offers some support for our speculation, however, when he says, "The word has nothing to do with retribution, but is about something that improves or educates, though by suffering."[71] Frankl writes, "But let me make it perfectly clear that in no way is suffering *necessary* to find meaning. I only insist that meaning is possible even in spite of suffering—provided, certainly, that the suffering is unavoidable."[72]

Elihu asserts more than this; he asserts that suffering serves a specific purpose of redemption. As the result of suffering, Elihu says of a person in 33:26: "Let him pray to Eloah and he accepts him and he sees his face. And he returns to man (לאנוש) his righteousness." As we have seen, logotherapy would take issue with the notion that suffering is a necessary condition. Nevertheless, logotherapy does share with Elihu the position that suffering in the past remains an integrated, significant, and meaningful part of a person's life by virtue of the manner in which the person has chosen to bear the suffering. To illustrate this point, Frankl tells the story of a fellow physician who consulted him because he could not overcome a feeling of despair following the death of his wife. Frankl shares the following dialogue:

> What would have happened, Doctor, if you had died first, and your wife would have had to survive you?" "Oh," he said, "for her this would have been terrible; how she would have suffered!" Whereupon I replied, "You see, Doctor, such a suffering has been spared her, and it was you who have spared her this suffering—to be sure, at the price that now you have to survive and mourn her." He said no word but shook my hand and calmly left my office. In some way, suffering ceases to be suffering at the moment it finds a meaning, such as the meaning of a sacrifice.[73]

Since for Frankl the meaning of every human life is unique, and since the uniqueness of every human life derives in part from its history, it follows

---

71. Boss, *The Book of Job*, 164.

72. Frankl, *Man's Search for Meaning*, 113; italics original. Frankl continues, "If it *were* avoidable, however, the meaningful thing to do would be to remove its cause, be it psychological, biological or political. To suffer unnecessarily is masochistic rather than heroic." Frankl, *Man's Search for Meaning*, 113; italics original.

73. Frankl, *Man's Search for Meaning*, 113.

for him that no part of the past, including suffering, could ever be voided of meaning. He explains his reasoning this way: "The possibilities that every person has exclusively for himself are just as specific as the possibilities presented by every historical situation in its peculiar singularity."[74] He continues, "Thus the various values merge to form a concrete task for the individual. That merging gives them the uniqueness whereby every man feels himself personally and validly addressed."[75] He concludes, "Until he learns what constitutes the singularity and uniqueness of his own existence, he cannot experience the fulfillment of his life task as something binding on him."[76]

Newsom provides additional information relevant to our hermeneutic. She tells us, "Almost every critic and commentator regards chapter 33, with its account of redemptive suffering, as presenting Elihu's most significant contribution to the Joban dialogue."[77] In order to demonstrate how Elihu's argument is new, Newsom first explains what both Job and his friends had in common with respect to their differing views. For the friends, a good person "endures suffering, is delivered by God, and enjoys a peaceful and prosperous life after deliverance."[78] Job, however, imagines that presenting his case before God would lead to "the climatic moment in which he is cleared and released by God."[79] For both Job and the friends, there is no meaning in the suffering as such; rather, the suffering is relieved with an end that holds meaning. As Newsom puts it, "The outcome of the narrative does not so much serve to integrate and give meaning to all that has come before as to enable it to be voided of significance—to be forgotten."[80]

Elihu's point of view is different. For him, the period of suffering is meaningful as part of the story that leads to redemption. As Boss puts it, "Suffering is to arouse people to their shortcomings, and to cause them to turn to God."[81] Moreover, as Newsom explains, Elihu imagines Job's suffering within a story that follows a defined schema. The elements of the schema include a prideful person receiving a warning from God in a

---

74. Frankl, *The Doctor and the Soul*, 105.
75. Frankl, *The Doctor and the Soul*, 105.
76. Frankl, *The Doctor and the Soul*, 105.
77. Newsom, *The Book of Job*, 211. See, also, Boss, 164.
78. Newsom, *The Book of Job*, 211.
79. Newsom, *The Book of Job*, 212.
80. Newsom, *The Book of Job*, 212.
81. Boss, *Human Consciousness of God*, 175.

dream. The person does not understand the warning and then is subjected to suffering. A mediator, human or angelic, is present either before or after the suffering. The prideful person then repents of pride and is restored.[82] For Elihu, as Newsom explains, "What matters is not the end in itself but the 'process time' of psychological transformation, from suffering to crisis of knowledge to restoration."[83] Moreover, in contrast to Job and the friends, "the end does not eclipse what went before. Every element that transpires remains of significance and is integrated into a story that is not merely recognized as a meaningful whole but that must be told to others."[84]

Again, there is a linear movement from Job and his friends who see past suffering voided by a present or future restoration, to Elihu who sees past suffering integrated as part of a schema of redemption, to logotherapy that sees past suffering as an integrated part of a life of meaning.

The Sapiential Nature Hymn

Elihu's final point of dialogue with logotherapy is found in the use of a novel genre that Newsom calls the "sapiential nature hymn" found in Job 36:24—37:13 (though the precise beginning and ending points are disputed).[85] In short, the purpose of the genre is to develop a sense of piety through the contemplation of both the beauty and the purpose of nature. Wisdom is the result of the development of this attitude. Newsom explains it this way: "To recite such a composition is to situate oneself in a disposition of piety ... it is to just such persons that God gives wisdom. Thus, the recitation of the hymn is both a reflection of and an instrument for the cultivation of a particular character."[86] The reason that this is so is because there is no real difference between the appreciation of nature's beauty and its larger meaning and purpose. In other words, it is beautiful because it fulfills meaning. In an example of the genre in Sirach, Newsom writes, "No sharp division exists between the pleasure that comes from describing the thing itself and in recounting its purposiveness within divine creation."[87]

---

82. Newsom, *The Book of Job*, 213–16.
83. Newsom, *The Book of Job*, 212.
84. Newsom, *The Book of Job*, 212.
85. Newsom, *The Book of Job*, 220.
86. Newsom, *The Book of Job*, 223.
87. Newsom, *The Book of Job*, 225.

Habel's translation shows this appreciation of the beauty of creation in a particularly clear way in 36:22–28:

> Behold, El is sublime in his power.
> What counselor can compare with him?
> Who appoints his way for him?
> Who says, "You created the wrong way?"
> Remember, then, to extol his creation
> That humans hail with song.
> All humanity has seen it,
> Mortals beheld it from afar.
> Behold, El is mighty, beyond our comprehension;
> The number of his years beyond our reckoning.
> He draws up drops from the sea;
> They distill as rain from his raincloud.
> They flow down from the clouds
> And shower on all humanity.[88]

Frankl's second way of finding meaning in life is "by experiencing something—such as goodness, truth, and beauty—by experiencing nature and culture or, last but not least, by experiencing another human being in his very uniqueness—by loving him."[89] He pursues this point when he attaches greater meaning to a greater emotional response evoked by nature. "The higher meaning of a given moment in human existence can be fulfilled by the mere intensity with which it is experienced."[90] Frankl even suggests that the experience of only one such event may provide meaning to a life as a whole. "Let us ask a mountain-climber who has beheld the alpine sunset and is so moved by the splendor of nature that he feels cold shudders running down his spine—let us ask him whether after such an experience his life can ever again seem wholly meaningless."[91] Frankl's answer, of course, is that it could not. He writes, "He would have to reply that it had been worth while living if only to experience this ecstatic moment."[92]

Elihu offers Job a dramatic change of perspective—from that of Job's own mode of discourse to that of divine purpose expressed through nature.[93] Newsom, however, raises the critical issue of whether or not it is

88. Habel, *The Book of Job*, 495–96.
89. Frankl, *Man's Search for Meaning*, 111.
90. Frankl, *The Doctor and the Soul*, 43.
91. Frankl, *The Doctor and the Soul*, 44. Frankl was a mountain climber.
92. Frankl, *The Doctor and the Soul*, 43.
93. Newsom, *The Book of Job*, 231.

appropriate, or possible, for a person in pain to experience this perspective. She suggests that it may be an evasion. She explains, "The genre itself has no place for the voice of grief and misery. The human voice that speaks is not allowed to speak of its own fear or pain but only of the glory of God manifest in nature."[94] Consequently, she imagines a genre that was not available to Job, a genre that contains both the painful emotion of the lament along with the perspective of the sapiential nature hymn. She reflects that if such a genre existed "then perhaps one would have the kind of speech that Job could not find for himself and that no one was able to offer him."[95]

Logotherapy offers just this kind of speech. Frankl's clinical technique of focusing attention on something meaningful despite the presence of something painful (that is, his technique of dereflection) is based on the noetic ability of self-transcendence. Moreover, Frankl himself found that it was possible for a person in pain to have this perspective. He reflects, "As the inner life of the prisoner tended to become more intense, he also experienced the beauty of art and nature as never before. Under their influence he sometimes even forgot his own frightful circumstances."[96] In other words, as the prisoner was able to perceive beauty in the world, the prisoner focused attention away from the ugliness of imprisonment. Said differently, the prisoner did not allow the ugliness of imprisonment to detract from beauty and meaning that could be found in the world independent of the imprisonment. Frankl continues, "If someone had seen our faces on the journey from Auschwitz to a Bavarian camp as we beheld the mountains of Salzburg with their summits glowing in the sunset, through the little barred windows of the prison carriage, he would never have believed that those were the faces of men who had given up all hope of life and liberty."[97] Here, both suffering and beauty combine and both serve as sources of meaning.

CONCLUSION

Job has experienced the pull of his will to meaning through these sections. In the wisdom poem of chapter 28, Job has begun to glimpse the difference between ultimate meaning and the meaning of the moment, a difference that was not present in chapter 3. Job engages in an existential self-analysis

---

94. Newsom, *The Book of Job*, 232.
95. Newsom, *The Book of Job*, 232.
96. Frankl, *Man's Search for Meaning*, 39.
97. Frankl, *Man's Search for Meaning*, 39–40.

from our perspective and once more is conscious of the categorical values he has realized in the past. He becomes conscious of the possibility that meaning expressed through these values may even be a future reality. Finally, Elihu appears and allows us to explore communication with the divine, or the spiritual unconscious, and to consider the role of pain and suffering as part of the human experience. Finally, the sapiential nature hymn offers Job a new perspective, one that uses the experiential value of natural beauty expressed through poetry to refocus his attention to wisdom (or meaning) despite his suffering. This is only possible through the activation of the noetic ability of self-transcendence, the theme that becomes central to the next movement.

6

Job and Frankl's Self-Transcendence

THIS CHAPTER COVERS THE shortest portion of the book of Job: chapters 38 to 42 that include the God speeches, Job's response, and the epilogue. From the point of view of a logotherapy hermeneutic, however, they are also the most important. The God speeches reveal the reality of ultimate meaning as defined by logotherapy. Armed with this knowledge, our hermeneutic sees the text setting up the basic existential question for the reader to answer. Frankl's pinnacle concept of self-transcendence comes to the foreground as Job is restored in the epilogue.

Commentators hold a variety of opinions regarding the critical aspects of each of the two God speeches and the relationship of each to the rest of the book. Newsom explains that her reading of Job as a polyphonic text encounters a problem with the appearance of speech representing the voice of God. "When God speaks, it tends to bring conversation to an end," she notes.[1] However, she explains that the ambiguity and obliqueness of the speeches do not result in closing the conversation and that the conversation continues, howbeit more indirectly, following them. Our logotherapy hermeneutic thus becomes a continuation of that conversation.

---

1. Newsom, *The Book of Job*, 234.

THE GOD SPEECHES (JOB 38:1—41:26): ULTIMATE MEANING

Yahweh appears in chapter 38 and delivers a set of speeches, the first running from 38:1 to 40:2 and the second running from 40:6 to 41:26 (Eng. 41:34) with a brief statement by Job separating them.[2] Our logotherapy hermeneutic sees in these speeches evidence of what Frankl calls ultimate meaning. Ultimate meaning is described by Frankl as "a world beyond" the human world.[3] By recognizing the presence of ultimate meaning, logotherapy is able to offer a unique perspective on suffering different from that of other psychotherapeutic approaches in a way somewhat similar to the difference in perspective between the God speeches and the "therapeutic" approach of the friends. Cox, who has been reading Job from the point of view of the absurd, makes a similar point. He notes that the Book of Job is able to do what other absurd dramas cannot. Other dramas, and he names Beckett's *Trilogy* and Camus's *La Chute*, reach the end of human reason and recognize that they can go no further without something from outside the human experience entering. Only in the Book of Job does this actually happen. "Thus the Theophany," writes Cox, "is what carries the drama *Job* beyond anything the theatre of the absurd could reach."[4] Likewise, logotherapy with its understanding of ultimate meaning is able to hear the God speeches within this context.

Job 38:1a begins the first speech: "Then Yahweh answered Job out of the tempest." Logotherapy notes that it is Yahweh who answers Job. A great deal of discussion could be spent on divine names in the book of Job, a complete topic unto itself, but for a logotherapy hermeneutic, the use of the personal name of God, related to the verb "to be," suggests to a logotherapist that God is speaking to the noetic and existential dimension of Job, not the psychological and rational dimension. Boss provides some support for this notion when he says that the use of the divine name "conveys some sense of pure being, existence."[5] Perhaps even more to the point, LaCocque

---

2. This brief statement is a silencing of Job. The critical importance our hermeneutic gives to Job's final reply far outweighs it. Therefore, our hermeneutic sees it as mainly a tool to separate the two God speeches.

3. Frankl, *The Will to Meaning*, 145.

4. Cox, *The Triumph of Impotence*, 113; italics original.

5. Boss, *Human Consciousness of God*, 184. For a fuller discussion of this topic, see Gordis, *The Book of Job*.

notes that Yahweh speaks of El's creation.[6] He explains, "Consequently, we leave the level of religion or philosophy for the one of the existential I-Thou relationship where both partners of the covenant are affected by events lived in common."[7] In developing his rational arguments, Job called upon El-Shaddai to answer him. The rational arguments failed. El-Shaddai does not answer. Yahweh does.

The word סערה, or tempest, also deserves note. This is especially so in light of our earlier understanding of Job's turmoil in chapter 3 as being the result of the existential vacuum, a kind of noogenic neurosis. Derived from the root verb סער that means "to storm," or "to rage," the word is variously translated tempest, whirlwind, or storm-wind. Though the word may refer to actual weather, it need not, as its use in 9:17 suggests: "For with a tempest (a rage?) he crushes me and he multiplies my wounds without cause." So then, the turmoil Job experienced in chapter 3 may be thought of as the result of the divine tempest (or rage?) used to crush him. Tempest, for logotherapy then, also serves as a signifier for Frankl's concept of the existential vacuum itself, an emptiness (or rage?) within Job that resulted in his turmoil and out of which God now speaks to Job. Boss notes that throughout the Hebrew Bible, the סערה is something that only God creates and that only God can quiet. Like our logotherapy hermeneutic, he understands the tempest as a disturbance that causes a powerful psychological effect.[8] Indeed, Boss states, "the disturbance is in Job."[9]

"Who is this?" queries God in 38:2a. A logotherapist notes much in this simple question. "Who is this?" is the existential question for logotherapy. Who will Job choose to be in the face of a world of unjust suffering? The question is not only asked directly by God in the opening statement, it is elaborated upon in a way reminiscent of Frankl's own insight. That is, in 38:3b God continues, "I will question you and you will answer me." Frankl writes, "Ultimately, man should not ask what the meaning of his life is, but rather he must recognize that it is *he* who is asked. In a word, each man is questioned by life; and he can only answer to life by *answering for* his own

---

6. Yahweh makes reference to creation by El, Elohim, Eloah, or Shaddai in 38:7, 38:41, 39:17, 40:2, 40:9 and 40:19. For a fuller discussion of this topic, see LaCocque, "Impotence of Religion and Philosophy," 37–39.

7. LaCocque, "Impotence of Religion and Philosophy," 42.

8. Boss, *Human Consciousness of God*, 184.

9. Boss, *Human Consciousness of God*, 185.

life; to life he can only respond by being responsible.[10] Boss agrees when he writes, "Job has been concerned with what God has done, but now he must face up to himself, not passing on responsibility."[11] The way that Job answers this question, the way that Job becomes responsible, is the key to our logotherapy hermeneutic. Before we address it, however, there is more to note in the God speeches.

God describes Job has having spoken "words without knowledge" (38:2b). In our earlier discussion of chapter 3, we noted that Job's existential turmoil was the result of Job wedding his sense of meaning to his ability to understand *ultimate* meaning, something beyond human understanding. Our hermeneutic understands this description of Job in that light. Job did not and cannot know ultimate meaning; as long as ultimate meaning remains the only source of meaning he recognizes, his existential vacuum is inevitable. He is enraged at injustice he cannot comprehend and this produces his turmoil. God next proceeds to reveal a series of images of ultimate meaning that demonstrate the human person's inability to grasp it.

We have noted that ultimate meaning refers to a "a world beyond."[12] Rather than rational arguments, we find in the God speeches descriptive images that stir the imagination and the emotions. Newsom notes that they "engage specifically aesthetic dimensions of understanding."[13] Robert Gordis calls them "poetic pictures rich in hyperbole."[14] In this sense, they are almost dreamlike, with locations and creatures that fall outside waking human experience. In fact, since the tempest out of which God speaks is taken by our hermeneutic to be interior to Job, perhaps even reflective of a dream or vision, then our logotherapy hermeneutic may draw on existential dream analysis for guidance. As Newsom notes, "Only primary images can evoke the necessary recognition and emotional response."[15] Dream analysis in logotherapy, like in psychoanalysis, is based on free association to primary images.[16] The main difference compared to Freud's approach is that existen-

---

10. Frankl, *Man's Search for Meaning*, 109; italics original.
11. Boss, *Human Consciousness of God*, 185.
12. Frankl, *The Will to Meaning*, 145.
13. Newsom, *The Book of Job*, 236.
14. Gordis, *The Book of God and Man*, 119.
15. Newsom, *The Book of Job*, 248.
16. In Freudian analysis, primary processes refer to images and feeling states that arise from the unconscious. By definition, these processes are pre-verbal. Secondary processes are conscious and verbal. See Freud, *The Interpretation of Dreams*, 519–20 and 535–36.

tial dream analysis in logotherapy seeks to uncover unconscious spiritual elements in the dream rather than instinctual elements.[17] Some variation may be permitted, however, when applying such a technique to a text rather than to an actual dream. Associations will need to be inferred from words or themes previously used in the text, or by word pairing.

A dream association based on words previously used in the text, for example, is the land of "waste and desolation," שׁוֹאָה וּמְשׁוֹאָה, used before in 30:3 and now repeated in the imagery of 38:27. For Job, this place is outside his normal experience; it is a place for outcasts. While perhaps not entirely "a world beyond" the human world since social outcasts inhabit it, it is certainly a world beyond Job's world. Commentators focus their attention on the outcasts themselves, those diametrically opposed to Job in social status. Whereas Job held an honored position in society, the outcasts are rejected by it.[18] In dream imagery, however, the desolate land itself becomes symbolic of Job's rejection. Reversing the meaning of the symbol in the God speeches, this same land is cared for by God (38:25–27). The desolate land that Job fears (representing his turmoil?) is suddenly brought life-giving rain for God cuts "a channel for the torrents of rain" (38:25) and brings "rain . . . on the desert" (38:26). In our earlier example of an existential dream analysis—the ascent of the health care rocket—an analysis suggested that the spiritual unconscious was preparing the dreamer for a return to spiritual health. A similar interpretation may apply here. The land of "waste and desolation" in Job's spiritual unconscious is being transformed.

The multiple contrasts between domestic and wild animals provide another association that reinforces the reality of a "world beyond," an ultimate reality. Many of the contrasts have to do with the freedom of wild animals. For example, "Who let the wild donkey go free and who loosened the bonds of the swift donkey?" (39:5); "Is the wild ox willing to serve you? Will it spend the night at your manger?" (39:9); "Is it at your command that the eagle soars and makes its nest on high?" (39:27). Other examples have to do with the evident relish with which animals serve their purposes: "The wings of ostriches wave proudly" (39:13a); the horse "laughs at fear and is not dismayed and from the sword he does not turn back" (39:22). These contrasts underscore characteristics of freedom and purpose, key concepts in logotherapy. An existential dream analysis may assert that Job's spiritual

---

17. Frankl, *Man's Search for Ultimate Meaning*, 47.

18. See, for example, Habel, *The Book of Job*, 418–19 and Newsom, *The Book of Job*, 187–89 among others.

unconscious is here reinforcing these attitudes for him as part of his return to spiritual health.

The third example is an association with a previous theme, and it is one that goes to the heart of Job's existential vacuum. In chapter 3, Job sought to reverse creation itself. His curse had been, "Let those who curse a day curse it, who are skilled in rousing Leviathan" (3:8). Here, in a sense, God grants that request, though not in the way that Job imagined. Most creation narratives begin with symbols of chaos and tell of God establishing order. In chapters 38 and 39, the images move in the opposite direction and in a way that associates God with chaos.[19] It is God who rouses Leviathan and who seems to take a special pride in it: "Lay your hands on him! Think of the battle—you will not do it again! Hope [to do so] has been deceptive. Even at the sight of him, [one] is overpowered. No one is so fierce that he dares to rouse him. Who then can stand before me?" (40:32—41:2 Eng. 41:8–41:10).[20] Perhaps we have a sense of one of Job's nightmares here. Job has been given a glimpse behind the curtain of the existential vacuum and seen that God is also master of chaos in some way that Job can only understand existentially and symbolically, though hardly rationally. Job has caught a glimpse of "a world beyond."

Cox strikes a somewhat similar note: "It can be seen that Yahweh has raised the whole argument to the cosmic level, as Job had done in chapter 3."[21] Cox asserts that following this presentation of the reversal of creation, Job learns "he is not alone in the cosmos—he is not even central to it."[22] He explains, "Since he does not know the origins or the originator of things he cannot *know* creation, he can at most guess."[23] Cox continues, "Much less can he know the purpose, or know even if there is a purpose."[24] Newsom notes, "More disturbingly, it seems to associate God in a positive fashion with these creatures of the fearful beyond."[25] One speech even ends with the chilling provision of food for the vulture—the blood of slain human beings.

---

19. Newsom, *The Book of Job*, 247–48.

20. Translation difficulties in this passage are numerous. For further discussion see Gordis, *The Book of Job*, 567–68 and Habel, *The Book of Job*, 554–55.

21. Cox, *The Triumph of Impotence*, 132.

22. Cox, *The Triumph of Impotence*, 127.

23. Cox, *The Triumph of Impotence*, 126; italics original.

24. Cox, *The Triumph of Impotence*, 126.

25. Newsom, *The Book of Job*, 245.

"Man is incapable of understanding the ultimate meaning of human suffering," Frankl writes.[26] "We do not catch hold of it on intellectual grounds but on existential grounds, out of our whole being."[27] To illustrate his point further, Frankl uses the analogy of an ape repeatedly being injected as part of the process used to develop the polio vaccine. Although the virtual eradication of polio in the human species is a laudable outcome, Frankl notes that the ape "is not able to grasp the meaning of its suffering, for . . . it cannot enter into the world of man, the only world in which its suffering is understandable."[28] Frankl asserts that, likewise, human suffering can only be understood from the point of view of a world that the human person may not enter rationally. The divine speeches, then, serve to demonstrate the presence of an ultimate reality in a way that transcends human reason. Though it cannot be comprehended, its presence is made real for Job through the images shared with him by God.

For logotherapy, the purpose of existential dream analysis is "to lift not only instinctual but also spiritual phenomena into consciousness—and into responsibleness."[29] Therefore, we must ask two questions: What spiritual phenomenon has Job become conscious of? What responsibility has Job become conscious of? First, we may say that Job is now conscious that an ultimate meaning exists. This is reflected especially in the references to Behemoth and Leviathan, understood as primary images that transcend rational understanding. In logotherapy, as we have seen, the presupposition of ultimate meaning is a precondition to the meaningfulness of human life. This separates logotherapy from existential positions that deny ultimate meaning.[30] As Frankl puts it, "Human cognition is not of kaleidoscopic nature. If you look into a kaleidoscope, you see only what is inside of the kaleidoscope itself. On the other hand, if you look through a telescope you see something which is outside the telescope itself."[31] Job has been given a peek through the telescope. Now he knows there is something more; logotherapy says that he has become responsible to that something more.

---

26. Frankl, *The Will to Meaning*, 145.

27. Frankl, *The Will to Meaning*, 145.

28. Frankl, *The Will to Meaning*, 144–45.

29. Frankl, *Man's Search for Ultimate Meaning*, 47.

30. As one example, Frankl notes that logotherapy is opposed to the notion that the human person invents herself or himself, as asserted by Jean-Paul Sarte. See Frankl, *Man's Search for Meaning*, 60–61.

31. Frankl, *The Will to Meaning*, 60.

Second, the concepts of freedom and purpose have been raised to consciousness through the images of animals that exhibit these traits. Moreover, these are traits that God seems to especially admire in these animals, much as God admired Job's wholeness and integrity in the prologue. For our logotherapy hermeneutic, it is not unusual that such values would be revealed in dreamlike material. Writing of such concepts, Frankl notes that they "cannot be espoused and adopted by us on a conscious level—they are something that we *are*."[32] Job is now conscious of these concepts. He is conscious of who he is. He has the freedom to choose his response to this understanding.

Third, Job has become conscious that transformation is taking place within him. This we interpret from the image of the desolate land suddenly being brought rain and consequently blooming. A spiritual blooming is about to take place for Job; the spiritual unconscious is making him aware of it in these images. Frankl asserts: "Everyone has his own specific vocation or mission in life to carry out a concrete assignment which demands fulfillment. Therein he cannot be replaced, nor can his life be repeated. Thus, everyone's task is as unique as is his specific opportunity to implement it."[33] "I will question you and you will answer me" (38:3b). We stated that how Job answers this question, the way that Job becomes responsible, is the key to our logotherapy hermeneutic. Knowing the reality of ultimate meaning, Job is now ready to answer life. Job is ready to carry out his specific, concrete task.

JOB'S RESPONSE (JOB 42:1–6): THE FREEDOM TO CHOOSE

Job's response of 42:5–6 is the most important statement in the book for our logotherapy hermeneutic. Strangely, if not ironically, it is also one of the most difficult to translate and understand. According to B. Lynne Newell, scholars have historically agreed that Job either repents, relents, or changes his attitude. This remains the case even among scholars who believe that Job could not have repented based on his statements in the dialogue. It has, therefore, been seen by some as a later addition, or even as hypocritical.[34] A new view was advanced by John B. Curtis in 1979, who

32. Frankl, *Man's Search for Meaning*, 45; italics original.
33. Frankl, *Man's Search for Meaning*, 108–9.
34. Newell, "Job: Repentant or Rebellious?," 441.

translated the verse as a rejection of God. His translation reads, "Therefore I feel loathing contempt and revulsion (toward you, O God); and I am sorry for frail man."³⁵ The crux of the translation problem, according to Curtis, is found in the phrase על כן אמאס that is a Qal imperfect lacking an object. According to Curtis, previous translators have either supplied an object (for example, "I reject my riches") or used "myself" or "my life" as an object. Curtis argues that the verb can stand without an object; in this case Curtis understands it to refer to the God speeches that have just been presented.³⁶

Curtis's view informs Michel's translation that omits an object in favor of ellipses.³⁷ Michel argues that the suffix "-kā" (you) found in the verbs שמעתיך and ראתך form a vertical parallelism with the verbs אמאס and ונחמתי that are also parallel to each other. Michel explains, "The *vertical* pairing . . . strongly suggests that the . . . suffix does double duty also for the *horizontal* pair. . . . When the text is read aloud, with an emphasis on -*kā!*, 'YOU,' then there is simply no problem recognizing the intent of the poet."³⁸

Our logotherapy hermeneutic sees these verses as the third response of Job. The first two responses, we may recall, occurred after the two tests of the prologue. Job's response in 1:21 is "Yahweh has given and Yahweh has seized; the Name of Yahweh be blessed." The second response is in 2:10: "We have been receiving good from Elohim, but shall we not receive evil?" Based on Curtis and Michel, our translation of Job's third response is:

By the hearing of the ear, I had heard of you.	לשמע אזן שמעתיך
And now my eye has seen you.	ועתה עיני ראתך
Therefore, I reject . . .	על כן אמאס
And I pity . . .	ונחמתי
Upon dust and ashes.	על עפר ואפר

As Newsom notes, "Since the adversary's challenge, the reader has been waiting to see if Job will indeed curse God to God's face. What had been a figure of speech now becomes a literal possibility."³⁹ The difference

---

35. Curtis, "On Job's Response," 497–511.

36. Curtis, "On Job's Response," 501–2.

37. Michel, "Did Job or God Repent?," 5. Borrowing from Ugaritic, Michel also considers a possible translation of the final sentence, על עפר ואפר, as "a suckling of Dust-and-Dirt." Michel, "Did Job or God Repent?," 5.

38. Michel, "Did Job or God Repent?," 5; italics and capitalization original.

39. Newsom, *The Book of Job*, 237.

between the first two responses and the final response is that Job now has knowledge of an ultimate meaning, of "a world beyond" his own. For logotherapy this demands responsibility. Job has become conscious of his freedom and his purpose. The question is not will Job curse God, the real question is whether the reader will curse God in light of all that has just been read. The difficulty of the Hebrew forces the reader to stop. The ellipses present themselves. With the "-*kā*" of the previous lines still ringing in her ears, the reader must choose to curse God, adding the "-*kā*" if only in her mind, or to refrain. To pose the question otherwise is to fall into the trap of the friends, namely, the trap of psychologism that it is the task of logotherapy to avoid. What will the reader choose?

Of course, all that has just been read is in no way a unified voice. As was pointed out earlier, a reader is likely to find voices that she resonates with and other voices that she does not. What has happened through the literary device of the speeches of God, however, is to serve to collapse the various human voices over against what we have called ultimate meaning. The reader is, thus, challenged to find her own human voice in choosing how to read the ellipses. This position is similar, though not identical, to Newsom's view. The difference is that Newsom sees the monologue of Job as representing the human position vis-à-vis the divine position presented in the God speeches. Our hermeneutic sees the human position as including all the prior positions, collapsed to such an extent that their differences seem insignificant compared to the ultimate.[40]

Scheler's "stratification of the emotional life" is highly significant to a logotherapy hermeneutic at this point. Scheler proposes levels of feeling based on the degree to which they can be influenced by outside forces or stimuli. The deepest of the feelings and "the least 'reactive' feelings are . . . the *bliss and despair* of the person himself."[41] What Scheler means is that a basic attitude toward life is characteristic of a given person independent of events in the external world. As Scheler puts it: "For it is the *being and the self-value of the person himself* that is the 'foundation' of bliss and despair."[42] He elaborates, "Just as in despair there lies at the core of our personal experience and world an emotional 'No!' without our 'person' becoming a mere object of reflection, so also in 'bliss,' at the deepest level of the feeling of

---

40. For clarification of her viewpoint, see Newsom, *The Book of Job*, 238–39.
41. Scheler, *Formalism in Ethics*, 337; italics original.
42. Scheler, *Formalism in Ethics*, 344; italics original.

Job and Frankl's Self-Transcendence

happiness, there lies an emotional 'Yes!' Bliss and despair appear to be the correlates of the moral value of our personal being."[43]

This comes from the book that Frankl carried with him "like a bible."[44] It is, therefore, not coincidental that the original title of Frankl's book describing life in the concentration camps is *Trotzdem Ja Zum Leben Sagen: Ein Psychologe Erlebt das Konzentrationslager* (*Saying Yes to Life in Spite of Everything: A Psychologist Experiences the Concentration Camp*).[45] In commenting on the original title, Frankl explains that it "presupposes that life is potentially meaningful under any conditions, even those which are most miserable. And this in turn presupposes the human capacity to creatively turn life's negative aspects into something positive or constructive."[46] In other words, Frankl recognizes that blessing and cursing, or bliss and despair, are interpretive rather than objective.

Of Frankl's three categorical values (the creative, the experiential, and the attitudinal), the attitudinal value is the greatest. This is the value similar to Scheler's deep emotional attitude of bliss or despair. Frankl said "yes to life" in what he calls "perhaps the deepest experience I had in the concentration camp."[47] Frankl's clothes had been taken, including his coat that contained the manuscript for the first book on logotherapy that was hidden in the lining. Frankl began to realize that perhaps nothing would survive him—no family (the experiential value of love) and no work (the creative value of his book). In place of his own clothes, he "inherited the worn-out rags of an inmate who had already been sent to the gas chamber." Frankl goes on to report, "Instead of the many pages of my manuscript, I found in a pocket of the newly acquired coat one single page torn out of a Hebrew prayer book, containing the most important Jewish prayer, *Shema Yisrael*."[48] This discovery became a turning point for Frankl. Lacking the ability to fulfill meaning through the creative or experiential values, he fulfilled it through the attitudinal value. He writes, "How should I have interpreted

---

43. Scheler, *Formalism in Ethics*, 343.

44. Frankl, *Recollections*, 62.

45. Frankl, *Trotzdem Ja Zum Leben Sagen*, 1946. This book was first translated as *From Death-Camp to Existentialism* (1959) and later republished as *Man's Search for Meaning* (1962).

46. Frankl, *Man's Search for Meaning*, 137.

47. Frankl, *Man's Search for Meaning*, 114.

48. Frankl, *Man's Search for Meaning*, 115.

such a 'coincidence' other than as a challenge to *live* my thoughts instead of merely putting them on paper?"[49]

Frankl tells us, "Between stimulus and response there is a space. In that space is our power to choose our response. In our response lies our growth and our freedom."[50] This resonates well with what Newsom has noted. For her, the verses in question serve as a Bakhitinian loophole. That is to say, it "reserves the possibility of a word yet to be spoken."[51] She writes, "The disconnect between Job's framing of issues and God's reply . . . seems to create a sort of hermeneutical synaptic space."[52] In logotherapy, this "hermeneutical synaptic space," this space between stimulus and response, is where freedom of choice lies.

Unlike other commentators who see Job repenting, relenting, or rejecting, our logotherapy hermeneutic sees Job's response as deliberately unfinished, deliberately left open. The reader must choose to fill the ellipses, or not. The choice must be made even if life "has cast me into the mire and I have become like dust and ashes" (30:19), a condition not forgotten in Job's response. Logotherapy's dust and ashes, the tragic triad of pain, guilt, and death, remain as unavoidable in human life as ever. Life questions the reader just as God questions Job. The reader must now choose—does she choose "to curse God and die," or does she choose to "say 'Yes' to life in spite of everything." Our logotherapy hermeneutic does not choose for the reader. "Meaning cannot be given arbitrarily," Frankl writes, "but must be found responsibly."[53]

Frankl notes, "After all, it is not the function of logotherapy to give answers. Its actual function is rather that of a catalyst."[54] To serve this catalytic function, our logotherapy hermeneutic restates Frankl's categorical imperative as: Live as if you were already living for the second time, and had already cursed God before as you are about to do again.[55] To say yes to life means to realize the meaning of the moment through the categori-

---

49. Frankl, *Man's Search for Meaning*, 115; italics original.
50. Frankl, The Harvard Lectures, archive reference 19612.
51. Newsom, *The Book of Job*, 234.
52. Newsom, *The Book of Job*, 235.
53. Frankl, *The Will to Meaning*, 63.
54. Frankl, *The Will to Meaning*, 45.
55. Frankl's categorical imperative is: "Live as if you were already living for the second time and had acted as wrongly the first time as you are about to act now." Frankl, *The Feeling of Meaninglessness*, 89.

cal values simply because one makes the choice to do so. To say the same thing in the language of the Book of Job, it means to fear God and turn from evil, to choose disinterested piety—simply because one makes the choice to do so, makes the choice despite the inevitable suffering of life. Cox comes to a similar conclusion: "Man can be righteous in two ways: by keeping the commandments and the covenant, which is the common level of righteousness; and on a higher level by rejoicing in the will of Yahweh ... by recognizing that there is a divine purpose."[56] In this sense, we affirm our thesis that Job's final response represents an existential challenge to the reader that is nothing less than the existential challenge of life itself. That is, the challenge to discover meaning in life despite its suffering.

While our logotherapy hermeneutic affirms the existence of ultimate meaning, we nevertheless gain some insight here as to why Frankl insisted on a rigid boundary between the noetic dimension and the mind-body dimension. "The line between the spiritual and the instinctual cannot be drawn sharply enough," Frankl writes.[57] The human person can never experience ultimate meaning, just as Job never experienced cosmic creation, the foundations of the world. It remains "a world beyond." Newsom makes this point when she draws our attention to depictions of the boundaries of creation—the sea, the dawn, the storehouses of light and darkness. Only God can have a relationship with what is on either side of the boundary.[58] Only God can know this world and the world beyond. "Job and Leviathan emerge as paired opposites," she writes, "neither representing the full image."[59] Neither, therefore, is able to comprehend the whole.

THE EPILOGUE (JOB 42:7-17): SELF-TRANSCENDENCE

Throughout the dialogue, Job's friends advised him to pray to God. "If you return to Shaddai you will be rebuilt if you remove injustice from your tents," Eliphaz explains in 22:23. He continues, "You will make your prayer to him and he will hear you" (22:27a). Imagine the beauty of the scene

---

56. Cox, *The Triumph of Impotence*, 143.

57. Frankl, *Man's Search for Ultimate Meaning*, 32. For Frankl, this boundary serves to separate ultimate meaning from the meaning of the moment, the spiritual unconscious from the instinctual unconscious, and logotherapy from religion.

58. Newsom, *The Book of Job*, 244, 252.

59. Newsom, *The Book of Job*, 252.

in which Job does pray—but not for himself. He prays for his friends. In the end Job does exactly as his friends suggest, only with a higher purpose than they imagined. Frankl writes that "being human always points, and is directed, to something, or someone, other than oneself—be it a meaning to fulfill or another human being to encounter."[60] Cox makes a similar assertion: "Man . . . is not an autonomous part of nature, working out his own role in existence, but rather finding the meaning of it all outside himself."[61] Frankl calls this phenomenon self-transcendence and believes that it is the essence of existence.[62] From the viewpoint of logotherapy, by praying for his friends Job becomes more human and realizes his own best potential.[63]

A logotherapy hermeneutic can only understand Job's restoration in the epilogue from the position of self-transcendence. Frankl notes in this context the difference between self-transcendence and self-actualization. Had Job prayed for himself, for his own restoration, he would have been striving to actualize his own best potential. Frankl believes that this is impossible unless a person has someone or something else to live for. Frankl explains, "What is called self-actualization is not an attainable aim at all, for the simple reason that the more one would strive for it, the more he would miss it. In other words, self-actualization is possible only as a side-effect of self-transcendence."[64]

Job 42:10 says, "Yahweh returned the fortunes of Job when he had prayed for his friends and Yahweh added double to everything that belonged to Job." A logotherapy hermeneutic notices that Job's transcendence came before his fortunes were restored. The epilogue then tells us something about those fortunes. First, his brothers and sisters come to his house. They eat with him, expressing the experiential value of companionship;

---

60. Frankl, *Man's Search for Meaning*, 110.
61. Cox, *The Triumph of Impotence*, 145.
62. Frankl, *The Will to Meaning*, 50.
63. Frankl, *Man's Search for Meaning*, 111.
64. Frankl, *Man's Search for Meaning*, 111. Maslow defines self-actualization as "ongoing actualization of potentials, capacities and talents, as fulfillment of a mission (or call, fate, destiny, or vocation), as a fuller knowledge of, and acceptance of, the person's own intrinsic nature, as an unceasing trend toward unity, integration or synergy within the person." Maslow, *Toward a Psychology of Being*, 25. Frankl's position is that this actualization cannot be achieved "within the person" without someone or something outside of the person and toward which the person transcends. Frankl explains, "I wish to stress that the true meaning of life is to be discovered in the world rather than within man or his own psyche, as though it were a closed system." Frankl, *Man's Search for Meaning*, 110.

they comfort him, expressing the attitudinal value of sympathy; and they give him money, taken to be an expression of the creative value of work.

The last portion of the epilogue, 42:12–17, as did the prologue, describes a life that logotherapy considers full of meaning. The animals are doubled. As before, our logotherapy hermeneutic looks upon these domestic animals as related to the creative value, the result of Job's work or the capacity to do work. The daughters of Job are given special description in the text. Our logotherapy hermeneutic considers the daughters to reflect Job's capacity for love, an expression of the experiential value. Boss notes that their names are symbolic of the beauty of love, the beauty of the sacred, and physical beauty.[65] Finally, Job is given 140 years of life—double the human lifespan of 70 years referenced in Psalm 90. Boss notes, "It is as though this is the beginning of his life, a rebirth."[66] Although our logotherapy hermeneutic cannot draw a conclusion for the reader, at least we are given a hint that Job's attitudinal value, like Frankl's, had been to say yes to life, even if cast into dust and ashes. This double lifespan represents that choice.

Of course, a traditional, pious reading will see the epilogue as affirming Job's patience and righteousness, while a critical view will wonder if the retributive world view that seemed earlier to be critiqued is not reinstated. The logotherapy hermeneutic, however, sees the description of Job's physical restoration as symbolic of a much deeper noetic realization—namely, the realization that life may be affirmed and lived even though knowledge of the ultimate world beyond is lacking and, indeed, must be lived in this way if it is to be lived at all.

CONCLUSION

This chapter has seen Job discover the reality of ultimate meaning as reflected in the God speeches by being exposed to a world beyond his comprehension. His ambiguous response is left open in our logotherapy hermeneutic quite deliberately, as our hermeneutic believes this is the question being asked of us by the text. Finally, Job is restored to a meaningful life, replete with expressions of all of the categorical values. However, now

---

65. See Boss, *Human Consciousness of God*, 225, for how he arrives at this conclusion.

66. Boss, *Human Consciousness of God*, 226. Habel, on the other hand, notes in *The Book of Job*, 577, that Job lived 170 years after his affliction and died at the age of 240 according to the tradition recorded in the LXX. This would indicate that he had been 70 years old, the end of the normal human lifespan, at the time when his turmoil began.

these values are lived in the knowledge that ultimate meaning is also real. Job now has reason to assert along with logotherapy that "life never ceases to hold a meaning."[67]

---

67. Frankl, *The Will to Meaning*, 70.

7

The Eyes of a Child

WITH RESPECT TO THE limits of what can be said about ultimate meaning, Frankl became fond of telling the following story:

> A psychiatrist who goes beyond the concept of the super-meaning will sooner or later be embarrassed by his patients, just as I was when my daughter at about six years of age asked me the question, "Why do we speak of the *good* Lord?" Whereupon I said, "Some weeks ago, you were suffering from measles, and then the *good* Lord sent you a full recovery." However, the little girl was not content; she retorted, "Well, but please, Daddy, do not forget: in the first place he had sent me the measles."[1]

Frankl's daughter "was duly proud of being quoted so often. Only later it occurred to her that she never got an answer to her justified objection. So you see: the field is still wide open."[2] Although logotherapy remains

---

1. Frankl, *Man's Search for Meaning*, 118–19; italics original.
2. Vesely and Vesely-Frankl, personal communication, January 20, 2013. Frankl's daughter, Dr. Gabrielle Vesely-Frankl, kindly consented to providing more about her recollection of this incident through her husband, Dr. Franz Vesely: "As far as she remembers she must have been 5–6 years old when she had the measles. As every child, she liked the recompense for her sufferings in terms of additional attention by the parents. She was bedded in a central chamber with access both from father's drawing room and her own accustomed room, and one of them was always at hand. Well, once father came in and tried to comfort her with that wise advice, upon which she gave the precocious answer. He liked her independent way of bouncing the ball back to him, and he started to tell the story around, first to 'Uncle Paul' (Paul Polak, the other pioneer of Logotherapy) and then to others of his friends." Vesely and Vesely-Frankl, personal communication,

unable to answer the little girl's question, logotherapy nevertheless holds a unique position to enter into dialogue about meaning and suffering. This dialogue most often takes place behind the closed doors of private therapy offices and psychiatric clinics. At times, its principles are illustrated through the use of literature and other forms of expression, leading to the development of a proto-hermeneutic that is consciously non-critical and that speaks from the privileged position of its own philosophy of life.[3] Now, however, logotherapy and existential analysis has emerged as a considered and deliberate hermeneutic with the ability to engage in critical dialogue. A logotherapy hermeneutic is a species of special existential analysis as defined by Frankl.[4] It is a postmodern, practical philosophy that maintains its own point of view and yet is able to closely engage with a text. It is natural that the Book of Job, a text that deals with unjust suffering, be its first such dialogue partner.

Key issues for a logotherapy hermeneutic become evident through this dialogue. When reading the prologue and the dialogue, Frankl's concept of the existential vacuum and logotherapy's related rejection of reductionism, nihilism, and psychologism are central to a logotherapy understanding. Frankl's concepts of the categorical values—the ways that meaning can be discovered through doing, experiencing, and choosing—come to the foreground when the wisdom poetry and Job's monologue are read. The God speeches are understood through a logotherapy optic to involve the resolution of the existential vacuum by positing a difference between ultimate meaning and the meaning of the moment. Frankl's notion of self-transcendence concludes the key elements when the epilogue is read.

The first movement in the Book of Job, as a logotherapy hermeneutic sees it, is the overcoming of reductionism, nihilism, and psychologism. A logotherapy hermeneutic sees reductionism as represented by the satan, who asserts that Job's choices are neither authentic nor free. Rather, his choices are determined by the hedge of protection God has put around him, caused, in the vocabulary of psychology, by the environment. Job's refusal to curse God in his first two responses dismisses this argument. A variation of it appears, however, in the character of Job's wife who recommends death

---

January 20, 2013.

3. See, for example, Atlas, "Logotherapy and the Book of Job," 29–33; and Leslie, *Jesus and Logotherapy*, 7.

4. For discussion of general and special existential analyses, see Frankl, *The Doctor and the Soul*, 176.

and who, therefore, represents nihilism in our hermeneutic. This position, too, is rejected. Job nevertheless falls into turmoil, a state of noogenic neurosis, as the result of existential vacuum, a sense of meaninglessness. His friends represent psychologism in their attempt to give Job a meaning for his suffering. Although logotherapy resonates with many of their points, logotherapy understands that meaning cannot be given but can only be discovered responsibly by the sufferer. In rejecting the arguments of the friends, Job rejects psychologism and moves toward the discovery of his own meaning, even if the meaning he discovers is contrary to the teachings of society.[5]

In the second movement, Job reignites his will to meaning through meditation on wisdom. The poetry of the section speaks to the meaning of the moment through the creative, experiential, and attitudinal values. Job engages in an existential self-analysis and returns to consciousness previous meanings responsibly fulfilled. Through the use of the categorical values, logotherapy provides a hermeneutic that is able to hold both the beauty of nature and the pain of suffering together as avenues for the discovery of meaning. Frankl writes, "In camp, too, a man might draw the attention of a comrade working next to him to a nice view of the setting sun shining through the tall trees of the Bavarian woods (as in the famous watercolor by Dürer), the same woods in which we had built an enormous, hidden munitions plant."[6] Job remains unsatisfied, however. He perceives that meaning in life is in some way dependent upon an ultimate meaning,

---

5. The close agreement between logotherapy and the psychologism of the friends of Job is worrisome from the point of view of clinical practice. A logotherapy hermeneutic serves as a warning to logotherapists to avoid reducing any sufferer to the simple understanding offered by any psychological theory, even if that theory is logotherapy itself. Just as Frankl did when developing logotherapy, current and future logotherapists must be willing to authentically hear their patients; they must be sensitive to hearing the will to meaning that is expressed, even if that will to meaning runs counter to the framework of logotherapy.

6. Frankl, *Man's Search for Meaning*, 40. Frankl gives another example: "One evening, when we were already resting on the floor of our hut, dead tired, soup bowls in hand, a fellow prisoner rushed in and asked us to run out to the assembly grounds to see the wonderful sunset. Standing outside we saw sinister clouds glowing in the west and the whole sky alive with clouds of ever-changing shapes and colors, from steel blue to blood red. The desolate grey mud huts provided a sharp contrast, while the puddles on the muddy ground reflected the glowing sky. Then, after minutes of moving silence, one prisoner said to another, 'How beautiful the world *could* be!'" Frankl, *Man's Search for Meaning*, 40; italics original.

but has no way to separate his immediate, local experience (the meaning of the moment) from that of ultimate meaning.

The third movement provides this realization. God questions Job as life questions the reader. Images of the foundation of creation come to Job from out of the existential vacuum. He comes to acknowledge that an ultimate reality, an ultimate meaning, is real, although beyond his comprehension. This disconnection between God's world and Job's world leaves Job, and the reader, free to choose a response. As Frankl himself discovered, one is always free to say yes or no to life, or, in the language of the Book of Job, to curse God and die, or not, despite circumstances. "To be sure, a human being is a finite thing," Frankl writes, "and his freedom is restricted. It is not freedom from conditions, but it *is* freedom to take a stand toward conditions."[7] A space is presented to the reader to consider her choice. This is the attitudinal value. Once Job has found meaning through the attitudinal value, that is to say, in his freedom to choose his response, he then is capable of self-transcendence; he becomes responsible in a meaningful way toward the very friends who sought to reduce him.[8]

Cox provides some additional support for this conclusion. He explains, first, that Job's "basic premise was correct: the cosmos is, in man's experience, irrational and at times mindlessly cruel."[9] Second, however, Job learns that some ultimate order does exist. In the words of Cox, "Yahweh is not a God who takes away pain, or who carefully correlates the elements of existence so as to exhibit a pattern."[10] He continues, "He is essentially the 'something outside' that gives meaning to an absurd existence by the hope that there is an ultimate meaning, an ultimate plan. He does not show man the plan, for man could not comprehend it if he saw it."[11] Frankl would agree.

Logotherapy goes further than this, however, inasmuch as it provides a rationale for disinterested piety, the original challenge offered up by the satan. By separating ultimate meaning from the meaning of the moment, one is always able to discover meaning despite the lack knowledge. "What is

---

7. Frankl, *Man's Search for Meaning*, 130; italics original.

8. Boss, also, concludes that Job has gone through three different psychological stages. Our logotherapy reading differs from Boss's more general psychological reading in that it offers a theoretically consistent framework with which to understand these three states. See Boss, *Human Consciousness of Job*, 198.

9. Cox, *The Triumph of Impotence*, 152.

10. Cox, *The Triumph of Impotence*, 153.

11. Cox, *The Triumph of Impotence*, 153–54.

demanded of man is not, as some existential philosophers teach, to endure the meaninglessness of life, but rather to bear his incapacity to grasp its unconditional meaningfulness in rational terms," Frankl writes.[12] Indeed, from the viewpoint of logotherapy, meaning is unconditional and always available. Frankl says that "the meaning of life always changes, but that it never ceases to be."[13] By being responsible to his friends, Job has discovered meaning in the moment despite his inability to understand the ultimate meaning that spoke to him from out of the tempest. In other words, in the epilogue, Job's piety becomes one of choice in the moment rather than one based on future expectation as in the monologue.

Now that a logotherapy hermeneutic has been established, it is hoped that logotherapy will engage in critical ways with other pieces of literature. Qoheleth would make an interesting dialogue partner. One wonders what dialogue would emerge if logotherapy engaged a text that uses meaninglessness as a refrain and that describes wisdom (that we have closely associated with meaning and is the primary human motivation according to logotherapy) as "a striving after wind" (Qoh 1:17b). Contemporary works, such as *The Death of Ivan Ilych*, also provide potential dialogue partners as do the plays mentioned by Cox. As logotherapy reads other texts, different elements of the theory and therapy of Frankl would likely emerge as key elements in those dialogues, allowing a logotherapy hermeneutic to expand its repertoire of meaning discovery.[14]

Frankl's tragic triad of pain, guilt, and death are universal human experiences. They are reflected in the lives of all human beings, all of whom are sufferers in some way, and are central themes in much of the world's great sacred and classic literature. Not only does the voice of Viktor Frankl deserve to be heard in dialogue with these great works, his logotherapy and existential analysis provides a hermeneutic viewpoint for which there can be no substitute. If Frankl could speak to Job, I think he would say, "Bear

---

12. Frankl, *Man's Search for Meaning*, 118.

13. Frankl, *Man's Search for Meaning*, 111.

14. In his initial reading of *The Death of Ivan Ilych* from the perspective of logotherapy, Sadigh found key themes to include the existential vacuum, suffering, and the ability to restore meaning to a wasted life through choices made in the present. See Sadigh, "Transcending Inauthenticity, Meaningless, and Death," 82–88. Recall, too, that Frankl made reference to this novel when speaking to the prisoners at the California State Prison in San Quentin as reported in Frankl, *The Will to Meaning*, 76–77.

your suffering with such integrity and wholeness that God may, in fact, someday answer you."[15]

---

15. The warrant for this speculation comes from Frankl's case study of the rabbi who had lost his children as told in Frankl, *Man's Search for Meaning*, 119–20.

Bibliography

Adler, Alfred. *The Practice and Theory of Individual Psychology.* Translated by P. Radin. New York: Harcourt, Brace, 1924.
Atlas, Alan J. "Logotherapy and the Book of Job." *The International Forum for Logotherapy* 7 (1984) 29–33.
Bakhtin, Mikhail. *The Dialogic Imagination: Four Essays.* Edited by M. Holquist. Translated by C. Emerson and M. Holquist. Austin: University of Texas Press, 1981.
———. *Problems of Dostoevsky's Poetics.* Edited and translated by C. Emerson. Theory and History of Literature 8. Minneapolis: University of Minnesota Press, 1986.
Barnes, Robert C. *Franklian Psychology and Attitudinal Change.* Edited by George E. Rice and developed by Paul Welter. Abilene, TX: Viktor Frankl Institute of Logotherapy, 1995, 2006.
———. *Franklian Psychology: An Introduction to Logotherapy.* Edited by George E. Rice. Abilene, TX: Viktor Frankl Institute of Logotherapy, 2005.
———. *Franklian Psychology: Meaning-Centered Interventions.* Abilene, TX: Viktor Frankl Institute of Logotherapy, 2005.
Barr, James. "The Book of Job and Its Modern Interpreters." *Bulletin of the John Rylands Library* 54 (1971–72) 28–46.
Barton, John, ed. *The Cambridge Companion to Biblical Interpretation.* Cambridge: Cambridge University Press, 1998.
Batthyány, Alexander. Introduction to *The Feeling of Meaninglessness: A Challenge to Psychotherapy and Philosophy*, by Viktor E. Frankl, 7–39. Edited by Alexander Batthyány. Milwaukee: Marquette University Press, 2010.
———, ed. *Logotherapy and Existential Analysis: Proceedings of the Viktor Frankl Institute Vienna.* Vol. 1. Switzerland: Springer, 2016.
———. "Open Microphone Question and Answer Period." Lecture, Congress Vienna 2012: The Future of Logotherapy, Vienna, Austria, March 18, 2012.
Batthyány, Alexander, and Jay Levinson, eds. *Existential Psychotherapy of Meaning: Handbook of Logotherapy and Existential Analysis.* Phoenix: Zeig, Tucker & Theisen, 2009.
Ben-Barak, Zafrira. "The Daughters of Job." *Eretz-Israel* 24 (1995) 41–48.
Binswanger, Ludwig. "The Existential Analysis School of Thought." In *Existence: A New Dimension in Psychiatry and Psychology*, edited by Rollo May, Ernest Angel, and Henri F. Ellenberger, 191–213. New York: Clarion, 1958.
———. *Grundformen und Erkenntnis menschlichen Daseins* [Basic Forms and Realization of Human Existence]. 3rd ed. Zurich: Munich/Bâle, 1942, 1962.

Bibliography

Bishop, Paul. *Jung's "Answer to Job."* Hove: Brunner-Routledge, 2002.
Boss, Jeffrey. *Human Consciousness of God in the Book of Job: A Theological and Psychological Commentary.* New York: T. & T. Clark, 2010.
Camus, Albert. *The Myth of Sisyphus and Other Essays.* Translated by Justin O'Brien. New York: Vintage, 1955.
Ceresko, Anthony R. *Job 29-31 in the Light of Northwest Semitic: A Translation and Philological Commentary.* Biblica et Orientalia 36. Rome: Biblical Institute, 1980.
Corey, Gerald. *Theory and Practice of Counseling and Psychotherapy.* Pacific Grove, CA: Brooks/Cole, 1991.
Costello, Stephen J. *Hermeneutics and the Psychoanalysis of Religion.* New York: Lang, 2010.
Cox, Dermot. *The Triumph of Impotence: Job and the Tradition of the Absurd.* Analecta Gregoriana 212. Rome: Universita Gregoriana Editrice, 1978.
Crenshaw, James L. "Method in Determining Wisdom Influence upon Historical Literature." *Journal of Biblical Literature* 88 (1969) 129-42.
Curtis, John. "On Job's Response to Yahweh." *Journal of Biblical Literature* 98 (1979) 497-511.
Dell, Katharine J. *The Book of Job as Sceptical Literature.* Beihefte zur Zeitschrift für die alttestamentliche Wissenschaft 197. Berlin: de Gruyter, 1991.
Dick, Michael B. "Job 31, the Oath of Innocence, and the Sage." *Zeitschrift für die alttestamentliche Wissenschaft* 95 (1983) 31-53.
———. "The Legal Metaphor in Job 31." *Catholic Biblical Quarterly* 41 (1979) 37-50.
Eaton, John H. *Job.* Old Testament Guides. Sheffield: JSOT Press, 1985.
Fabry, Joseph B. Introduction to *Synchronization in Buchenwald*, by Viktor E. Frankl, 1. Vienna: copyright held by the family of Dr. Frankl, 1945.
———. *The Pursuit of Meaning.* Boston: Beacon, 1968.
Fabry, Joseph B., Reuven P. Bulka, and William S. Sahakian, eds. *Logotherapy in Action.* New York: Aronson, 1979.
Fohrer, Georg. *Das Buch Hiob.* Kommentar zum Alten Testament 16. Gütersloh: Gütersloher, 1963.
———. "The Righteous Man in Job 31." In *Essays in Old Testament Ethics*, edited by James L. Crenshaw and John T. Willis, 1-22. New York: Ktav, 1974.
Frankl, Viktor E. *The Doctor and the Soul.* 3rd ed. New York: Vintage, 1980.
———. *From Death-Camp to Existentialism: A Psychiatrist's Path to a New Therapy.* Boston: Beacon, 1959.
———. *The Feeling of Meaninglessness: A Challenge to Psychotherapy and Philosophy.* Edited by Alexander Batthyány. Milwaukee: Marquette University Press, 2010.
———. The Harvard Lectures. Vienna: The Viktor Frankl Archives, 1961.
———. *Man's Search for Meaning.* Boston: Beacon, 1959, 1984, 2006.
———. *Man's Search for Ultimate Meaning.* New York: Perseus, 2000.
———. *On the Theory and Therapy of Mental Disorders.* New York: Brunner-Routledge, 2004.
———. "Philosophie und Psychotherapie: Zur Grundlegung einer Existenzanalyse." *Schweizerische medizinische Wochenschrift* 69 (1939) 707-9.
———. "Psychotherapie und Weltanschauung: Zur grundsatzlichen Kritik ihrer Beziehungen." *Internationale Zeitschrift für Individualpsychologie* 3 (1925) 250-52.
———. *Psychotherapy and Existentialism: Selected Papers on Logotherapy.* New York: Simon & Schuster, 1985.

———. *Recollections: An Autobiography.* New York: Basic Books, 2000.
———. *Synchronization in Buchenwald.* Vienna: copyright held by the family of Dr. Frankl, 1945.
———. *Trotzdem Ja zum Leben Sagen: Ein Psychologe Erlebt das Konzentrationslager.* Vienna: Jugend und Volk, 1946.
———. *The Unconscious God: Psychotherapy and Theology.* New York: Simon & Schuster, 1985.
———. *The Unheard Cry for Meaning: Psychotherapy and Humanism.* New York: Simon & Schuster, 1985.
———. *The Will to Meaning.* Cleveland: World, 1969.
———. "Zur geistigen Problematik der Psychotherapie." *Zentralblatt für Psychotherapie* 10 (1938) 33–45.
Freud, Sigmund. *The Interpretation of Dreams.* In *The Basic Writings of Sigmund Freud.* Translated by A. A. Brill. New York: Random House, 1938.
———. *An Outline of Psycho-Analysis.* Translated by James Strachey. Rev. ed. New York: Norton, 1949, 1969.
Gadamer, Hans-Georg. "Hermeneutics and Logocentrism." In *Dialogue and Deconstruction: The Gadamer-Derrida Encounter,* edited by Diane P. Michelfelder and Richard E. Palmer, 114–25. Albany: State University of New York Press, 1989.
———. *Truth and Method.* Translated by William Glen-Doepel. Edited by John Cumming and Garrett Barden. London: Sheed & Ward, 1975.
———. "The Universality of the Hermeneutic Problem." In *Hermeneutical Inquiry,* edited by David E. Klemm, vol. 1, 179–82. AAR Studies in Religion 43. Atlanta: Scholars, 1986.
———. "What Is Practice? The Conditions of Social Reason." In *Hermeneutical Inquiry,* by David E. Klemm, vol. 2, 241–52. AAR Studies in Religion 44. Atlanta: Scholars, 1986.
Garfield, Sol L. *Psychotherapy: An Eclectic Approach.* New York: Wiley, 1980.
Gaster, T. H. "Leviathan." In *The Interpreter's Dictionary of the Bible,* edited by George Arthur Buttrick, 3:116. New York: Abingdon, 1962.
Gelber, S. Michael. *Job Stands Up.* New York: Union of American Hebrew Congregations, 1975.
Gordis, Robert. *The Book of God and Man: A Study of Job.* Chicago: University of Chicago Press, 1965.
———. *The Book of Job: Commentary, New Translation, and Special Studies.* New York: Jewish Theological Seminary of America, 1978.
Graber, Ann V. Personal telephone communication from board member of the Viktor Frankl Institute of Logotherapy, December 1, 2012.
———. *Viktor Frankl's Logotherapy: Method of Choice in Ecumenical Pastoral Psychology.* 2nd ed. Lima, Ohio: Wyndham Hall, 2004.
Greenberg, Moshe. *The Book of Job: A New Translation according to the Original Hebrew Text.* Philadelphia: Jewish Publication Society, 1980.
Gutiérrez, Gustavo. *On Job: God-Talk and the Suffering of the Innocent.* Translated by Matthew J. O'Connell. Maryknoll, NY: Orbis, 1987.
Habel, Norman C. *The Book of Job, A Commentary.* Old Testament Library. Philadelphia: Westminster, 1985.
———. "Wisdom in the Book of Job." In *Sitting with Job: Selected Studies on the Book of Job,* edited by Roy B. Zuck, 303–15. Grand Rapids: Baker, 1992.

Bibliography

Halling, Steen, and Judy Dearborn Nill. "A Brief History of Existential-Phenomenological Psychiatry and Psychotherapy." *Journal of Phenomenological Psychology* 26 (1995) 1–45.

Hallowell, David A. "LogoTalk Episode 22, Interview with David A. Hallowell." *LogoTalk Radio*, podcast audio (October 11, 2010). http://www.logotalkradio.com.

Hartley, John E. *The Book of Job*. New International Commentary on the Old Testament. Grand Rapids: Eerdmans, 1988.

Heidegger, Martin. *Being and Time*. Translated by Joan Stambaugh. Albany: State University of New York Press, 1996.

Holbert, John C. "The Rehabilitation of the Sinner: The Function of Job 29–31." *Zeitschrift für die alttestamentliche Wissenschaft* 95 (1983) 229–37.

Jung, Carl G. *Aion*. Translated by R. F. C. Hull. Collected Works of C. G. Jung 9. London: Routledge, 1958.

———. *Answer to Job*. Translated by R. F. C. Hull. Collected Works of C. G. Jung 11. Translated by R. F. C. Hull. London: Routledge, 1958.

———. *The Archetypes and the Collective Unconscious*. Translated by R. F. C. Hull. Collected Works of C. G. Jung 9. London: Routledge, 1958.

———. *The Structure of the Psyche*. Translated by R. F. C. Hull. Collected Works of C. G. Jung 8. London: Routledge, 1958.

Klemm, David E. *Hermeneutical Inquiry*. Vol. 1, *The Interpretation of Texts*. AAR Studies in Religion 43. Atlanta: Scholars, 1986.

———. *Hermeneutical Inquiry*. Vol. 2, *The Interpretation of Existence*. AAR Studies in Religion 44. Atlanta: Scholars, 1986.

Klingberg, Haddon. "Logotherapy, Frankl, and Positive Psychology." In *Existential Psychotherapy of Meaning: Handbook of Logotherapy and Existential Analysis*, edited by Alexander Batthyány and Jay Levinson, 197–223. Phoenix: Zeig, Tucker & Theisen, 2009.

LaCocque, André. "Job or the Impotence of Religion and Philosophy." In *Semeia 19: The Book of Job and Ricoeur's Hermeneutics*, edited by John Dominic Crossan, 33–52. Chico, CA: Scholars, 1981.

Leslie, Robert C. *Jesus and Logotherapy: The Ministry of Jesus as Interpreted through the Psychotherapy of Viktor Frankl*. New York: Abingdon, 1968.

Lukas, Elisabeth. *Logotherapy Textbook: Meaning-centered Psychotherapy Consistent with the Principles Outlined by Viktor E. Frankl, M.D.* Translated by Theodor Brugger. Toronto: Liberty, 2000.

Maslow, Abraham H. *Toward a Psychology of Being*. 2nd ed. New York: Van Nostrand Reinhold, 1968.

May, Rollo, Ernest Angel, and Henri F. Ellenberger, eds. *Existence: A New Dimension in Psychiatry and Psychology*. New York: Clarion, 1958.

Michel, Walter L. "Did Job or God Repent? Job 42:5–6: Ellipses and Janus Parallelism in Job's Final Response to an Abusive God and the Message of the Book of Job." Paper presented at the joint meeting of the Midwest Region of the Society of Biblical Literature, Wheaton, Illinois, February 1997.

———. *Job in the Light of Northwest Semitic*. Vol. 1. Biblica et Orientalia 42. Rome: Biblical Institute Press, 1987.

Moore, Rick D. "The Integrity of Job." *Catholic Biblical Quarterly* 45 (1983) 17–31.

Nemo, Philippe. *Job and the Excess of Evil*. Translated by Michael Kigel. Pittsburgh: Duquesne University Press, 1998.

Newell, B. Lynne. "Job: Repentant or Rebellious?" In *Sitting with Job: Selected Studies on the Book of Job*, edited by Roy B. Zuck, 441–56. Grand Rapids: Baker, 1992.

Newsom, Carol A. *The Book of Job: A Contest of Moral Imaginations*. Oxford: Oxford University Press, 2003.

Pope, Marvin. *Job: A New Translation with Introduction and Commentary*. 3rd ed. Anchor Bible 15. Garden City, NY: Doubleday, 1965.

Rad, Gerhard von. *Wisdom in Israel*. Translated by J. D. Martin. Nashville: Abingdon, 1972.

Redsand, Anna. *Viktor Frankl: A Life Worth Living*. New York: Clarion, 2006.

Rice, Cynthia Wimberly, and George E. Rice, eds. *Franklian Psychology: Theory and Therapy of Mental Disorders*. Abilene, TX: Viktor Frankl Institute of Logotherapy, 2005.

Ricoeur, Paul. "Existence and Hermeneutics." In *Hermeneutical Inquiry*, edited by David E. Klemm, vol. 2, 185–202. AAR Studies in Religion 44. Atlanta: Scholars, 1986.

———. *Freud and Philosophy: An Essay on Interpretation*. Translated by Denis Savage. New Haven: Yale University Press, 1970.

———. *Hermeneutics and the Human Sciences*. Edited and translated by John B. Thompson. Cambridge: Cambridge University Press, 1981.

———. "What Is a Text? In *Hermeneutical Inquiry*, edited by David E. Klemm, vol. 1, 233–46. AAR Studies in Religion 43. Atlanta: Scholars, 1986.

Roberts, J. J. M. "Job and the Israelite Religious Tradition." *Zeitschrift für die alttestamentliche Wissenschaft* 89 (1977) 107–14. Reprinted in Roberts, *The Bible and the Acient Near East: Collected Essays*, 110–16. Winona Lake, IN: Eisenbrauns, 2002.

Rogina, Julius M. "Editorial." *International Forum for Logotherapy* 33 (2010) 1–3.

Ryce-Menuhin, Joel. *A New Look at Jung's "Answer to Job."* Guild Lecture 237. London: Guild of Pastoral Psychology, 1991.

Sadigh, Micah. *Existential Journey: Viktor Frankl and Leo Tolstoy on Suffering, Death, and the Search for Meaning*. Lima, OH: Wyndham Hall, 2014.

———. "Transcending Inauthenticity, Meaninglessness, and Death: Literary Analysis through the Lens of Franklian Psychology." *International Forum for Logotherapy* 31 (2008) 82–88.

Sahakian, William S. "Logotherapy's Place in Philosophy." In *Logotherapy in Action*, edited Joseph B. Fabry et al., 53–59. New York: Aronson, 1979.

Sanders, Paul, ed. *Twentieth Century Interpretations of the Book of Job: A Collection of Critical Essays*. Englewood Cliffs, NJ: Prentice-Hall, 1968.

Scheler, Max. *Formalism in Ethics and Non-Formal Ethics of Values: A New Attempt Toward the Foundation of an Ethical Personalism*. Translated by Manfred S. Frings and Roger L. Funk. Evanston, IL: Northwestern University Press. 1973.

Schreiber, Andreas. *Konnektionismus und Heidegger: Versuch einer Vermittlung zwischen neuronalen Netztheorien und Heideggers spätphilosophischem Denken des Gevierts*. NoRa Science. Berlin: NoRa, 2001.

Snaith, Norman H. *The Book of Job: Its Origin and Purpose*. Studies in Biblical Theology 2/11. Naperville, IL: Allenson, 1968.

Soucek, W. "Die Existenzanalyse Frankls, die Dritte Richtung der Wiener psychotherapeutischen Schule." *Deutsche Medizinische Wochenschrift* 73 (1948) 594–95.

Spiegelberg, Herbert. *Phenomenology in Psychology and Psychiatry—A Historical Introduction*. Evanston, IL: Northwestern University Press, 1972.

BIBLIOGRAPHY

Spiegelman, J. Marvin. "C. G. Jung's Answer to Job: A Half Century Later." *Journal of Jungian Theory and Practice* 8 (2006) 1–18.

Steger, Michael F., Patricia Frazier, Shigehiro Oishi, Matthew Kaler. "The Meaning in Life Questionnaire: Assessing the Presence of and Search for Meaning in Life." *Journal of Counseling Psychology* 53 (2006) 80–93.

Storr, Anthony. *The Essential Jung*. Princeton: Princeton University Press, 1983.

Terrien, Samuel. "The Yahweh Speeches and Job's Response." *Review and Expositor* 68 (1971) 497–509.

Terrien, Samuel, and Paul Scherer. "The Book of Job." *The Interpreter's Bible*, edited by George Arthur Buttrick, vol. 3, 875–1198. Nashville: Abingdon, 1954.

Thayer, Joseph Henry. *The New Thayer's Greek-English Lexicon*. Peabody, MA: Hendrickson, 1979, 1981.

Thompson, John B. "Introduction." In *Hermeneutics and the Human Sciences*, by Paul Ricoeur, edited and translated by John B. Thompson, 1–26. Cambridge: Cambridge University Press, 1981.

Tilley, Terrence W. *The Evils of Theodicy*. Washington, DC: Georgetown University Press, 1991.

Tsevat, Matitiahu. "The Meaning of the Book of Job." *Hebrew Union College Annual* 37 (1966) 73–106.

Vesely, Franz, and Gabrielle Vesely-Frankl. Personal email communication, January 20, 2013.

Ward, William B. *Out of the Whirlwind: Answers to the Problem of Suffering from the Book of Job*. Richmond: John Knox, 1958.

Westphal, Merold. *Whose Community? Which Interpretation?: Philosophical Hermeneutics for the Church*. Grand Rapids: Baker Academic, 2009.

Williams, James G. "Deciphering the Unspoken: The Theophany of Job." *Hebrew Union College Annual* 49 (1978) 59–72.

———. "'You Have not Spoken the Truth of Me': Mystery and Irony in Job." *Zeitschrift für die alttestamentliche Wissenschaft* 83 (1971) 231–55.

Wolde, Ellen J. van. "Job 42:1–6: The Reversal of Job." In *The Book of Job*, edited by W. A. M. Beuken, 223–50. Bibliotheca ephemeridum theologicarum lovaniensium 114. Leuven: Leuven University Press, 1994.

Zamalieva, Snezhana. *Chelovek vse reshaet sam. Logoterapiya i ekzistentsialnaya antropologiya Viktora Frankla* [Man Decides for Himself: Viktor Frankl's Logotherapy and Existential Anthropology]. Saint Petersburg: University Books, 2012.

Zuck, Roy B., ed. *Sitting with Job: Selected Studies on the Book of Job*. Grand Rapids: Baker, 1992.

Index

Note: n indicates footnotes, and italicized page numbers indicate illustrations.

Abraham, 59
Academic Society for Medical Psychology, 10
Adler, Alfred, 10–13, 45
Allers, Rudolf, 13n71
American Embassy, 27
American psychology, logotherapy and, 14–16
anima, 35
Answer to Job (Jung), 3
answer to Jung, Frankl's, 13–14
applications of logotherapy
   clinical, 36–38
   hermeneutic, 55–56
areas of freedom vs. fate, 26, 57, 60
assumptions, Frankl's, 26–29
Atlas, Alan J., 17–19
attitudinal value
   application of a logotherapy hermeneutic, 55
   categorical values, 25–26
   eyes of a child, 120–22
   Job and Frankl's self-transcendence, 117
   Job and Frankl's will to meaning, 82

Job and the meaningful life, 59–62
Job's monologue and existential self-analysis, 91, 93
Job's response and the freedom to choose, 113
Job's turmoil in the existential vacuum, 64, 66–67
logotherapy and Job, 76–77, 79, 81
logotherapy and the friends of Job, 71, 73, 76
logotherapy of Job and his friends, 71
Auschwitz, 23, 101
Austria, 4, 17n94, 25, 27, 101
Austro-Hungarian Empire, 7

Baal, 68
Bakhtin, Mikhail, 9
Barnes, Robert C., 17
Barton, John, 53
Batthyány, Alexander, 4, 17, 21
Beckett, Samuel, 7, 104
Behemoth, 109
Being and Time (Heidegger), 19
Berlin, Germany, 23

Index

Bible, 42, 105
Bildad, 69–70, 74–75
Binswanger, Ludwig, 3–4, 13, 41, 44–45
The Book of Job (Habel), 117n66
Boss, Jeffrey
  Elihu's monologue, 94
  eyes of a child, 122n8
  God's speeches and ultimate meaning, 104–6
  Job and Frankl's existential vacuum, 57–58
  Job and Frankl's self-transcendence, 117
  Job's monologue and existential self-analysis, 89, 92
  Job's turmoil in the existential vacuum, 66
  Job's wisdom poem and will to meaning, 83, 88–89
  logotherapy and Job, 80
  place of past suffering, 97–98
  statement of Job's problem, 7, 10
  terrible paradox of suffering, 2
Boss, Medard, 41, 44
Buber, Martin, 34
Bulka, Reuven P., 16

California, 123n14
Camus, Albert, 7, 104
Capra, Fritjof, 15
categorical imperative of logotherapy, 36, 91, 114
categorical values
  about, 25–26
  application of a logotherapy hermeneutic, 55
  eyes of a child, 120
  Frankl's assumptions and will to meaning, 28
  Husserl on logotherapy and hermeneutics, 47
  Job and Frankl's self-transcendence, 117
  Job and Frankl's will to meaning, 82
  Job and the meaningful life, 59
  Job's monologue and existential self-analysis, 91–92
  Job's response and the freedom to choose, 113–15
  Job's wisdom poem and will to meaning, 85n15
  logotherapy and the friends of Job, 75–76
characteristics, demand, 27
child, eyes of a, 119–24
choice, freedom of, 26, 72, 81, 110–15
Christianity, 18, 42
clinical applications of logotherapy, 36–38
common roots of logotherapy and hermeneutics, 41–53
communication, divine, 82, 94–96
conscience, 34, 70, 77, 95–96
Costello, Stephen, 3
Cox, Dermot
  Elihu's monologue, 94
  eyes of a child, 122–23
  God's speeches and ultimate meaning, 104, 108
  Job and Frankl's existential vacuum, 57–58
  Job and Frankl's self-transcendence, 116
  Job's monologue and existential self-analysis, 89–90
  Job's response and the freedom to choose, 115
  Job's turmoil in the existential vacuum, 66, 68
  Job's wisdom poem and will to meaning, 83
  logotherapy and Job, 80
  statement of Job's problem, 7–8
creative value
  application of a logotherapy hermeneutic, 55
  categorical values, 25–26
  eyes of a child, 120–21
  Job and Frankl's existential vacuum, 57, 81
  Job and Frankl's self-transcendence, 117
  Job and Frankl's will to meaning, 82
  Job and the meaningful life, 59–62

INDEX

Job's monologue and existential self-analysis, 91, 93
Job's response and the freedom to choose, 113
Job's turmoil in the existential vacuum, 65, 67
Job's wisdom poem and will to meaning, 84
logotherapy and Job, 76–77, 79–80
logotherapy and the friends of Job, 71, 73, 76
logotherapy of Job and his friends, 71
Crenshaw, James L., 82
Curtis, John B., 110–11

Dasein, 43–44
Daseinsanalyse, 3–4, 13, 44–45
Daseinsanalytik, 44
The Death of Ivan Ilyich (Tolstoy), 19, 24, 123
demand characteristics, 27
dereflection, 37, 101
Dilthey, Wilhelm, 43
dimensional ontology, 29–33, 30, 47, 60
divine communication, 82, 94–96
The Doctor and the Soul: From Psychotherapy to Logotherapy (Frankl), 4, 11, 16
Dürer, Albrecht, 121

Eaton, John H., 6
Ebner, Ferdinand, 34
Elihu, 55, 82, 94–102
Eliphaz, 69–73, 78, 115
Existential Journey: Viktor Frankl and Leo Tolstoy on Suffering, Death, and the Search for Meaning (Sadigh), 19
The Existential Psychotherapy of Meaning: Handbook of Logotherapy and Existential Analysis (Batthyány), 4, 17
existential self-analysis, Job's, 82, 89–93, 101, 121
existential vacuum
of Frankl, 23–25, 55, 120, 123n14
of Job, 57–81, 105–6, 108, 121–22

Existenzanalyse, 3–4, 45
experiential value
application of a logotherapy hermeneutic, 55
categorical values, 25–26
eyes of a child, 120–21
Job and Frankl's existential vacuum, 57, 81
Job and Frankl's self-transcendence, 116–17
Job and Frankl's will to meaning, 82, 102
Job and the meaningful life, 59–62
Job's monologue and existential self-analysis, 90–91, 93
Job's response and the freedom to choose, 113
Job's turmoil in the existential vacuum, 65, 67
logotherapy and Job, 76–77, 79–80
logotherapy and the friends of Job, 71, 73, 76
logotherapy of Job and his friends, 71
eyes of a child, 119–24

Fabry, Joseph B., 16–17, 29
fate vs. freedom, areas of, 26, 57, 60
The Feeling of Meaninglessness: A Challenge to Psychotherapy and Philosophy (Batthyány), 4
First Force psychology, 14
first law of dimensional ontology, 31–32, 32
Formalism in Ethics (Scheler), 47
Fourth Force psychology, 14n82
Franklian Psychology, 4
freedom
areas of fate vs., 26, 57, 60
of choice, 26, 72, 81, 110–15
of the will, 26, 36, 46
Freud, Sigmund
clinical applications of logotherapy, 37
God's speeches and ultimate meaning, 106
Heidegger on logotherapy and hermeneutics, 44–45

Index

Freud, Sigmund *(continued)*
  logotherapy and Viennese psychiatry, 11–12
  nature of divine communication, 95–96
  nature of human person, 29–30
  spiritual unconscious, 33–34
  terrible paradox of suffering, 2–3

Gadamer, Hans-Georg, 41, 48–50
Germany, 11, 17, 23
Gestapo, 12
God
  application of a logotherapy hermeneutic, 55
  Elihu's monologue, 94
  eyes of a child, 119–20, 122, 124
  Frankl's answer to Jung, 14
  Job and Frankl's existential vacuum, 58
  Job and Frankl's self-transcendence, 103, 115–17
  Job and the meaningful life, 59–63
  Job's monologue and existential self-analysis, 90–93
  Job's response and the freedom to choose, 111–12, 114–15
  Job's turmoil in the existential vacuum, 64, 66, 68
  Job's wisdom poem and will to meaning, 83, 86–89
  logotherapy and Job, 76, 78–80
  logotherapy and the friends of Job, 71–76
  logotherapy of Job and his friends, 69
  nature of divine communication, 95–96
  place of past suffering, 97–98
  sapiential nature hymn, 99–101
  speeches of, 1, 8, 55, 75n88, 94, 103–12, 117, 120
  statement of Job's problem, 5–10
  terrible paradox of suffering, 1, 3
Gordis, Robert, 106
Graber, Ann V., 16
Greenberg, Moshe, 5
Grof, Stanislav, 15

Gutiérrez, Gustavo, 20–21

Habel, Norman C.
  Job and Frankl's self-transcendence, 117n66
  Job and Frankl's will to meaning, 83
  Job and the meaningful life, 59
  Job's turmoil in the existential vacuum, 67–68
  Job's wisdom poem and will to meaning, 83
  logotherapy and the friends of Job, 74–75
  sapiential nature hymn, 100
  statement of Job's problem, 6
Hallowell, David A., 16n93
hapax legomenon, 97
Hartley, John E., 6, 59, 64, 83
Hebron, Israel, 58
Heidegger, Martin, 4, 19, 41, 43–45, 51–52
Heraclitus, 48
hermeneutics
  application of logotherapy, 55–56
  and logotherapy, 39–56
  summary of logotherapy, 53–54
  toward logotherapy, 20–21
Holocaust
  existential vacuum, 23
  Frankl's logotherapy, 11, 22
  Job and the meaningful life, 62
  logotherapy and Viennese psychiatry, 12
  sapiential nature hymn, 101
  terrible paradox of suffering, 2
  toward a logotherapy hermeneutic, 20
human person
  clinical applications of logotherapy, 36–37
  common roots of logotherapy and hermeneutics, 43
  existential vacuum, 23
  Frankl's answer to Jung, 13
  Frankl's assumptions and will to meaning, 26–27
  God's speeches and ultimate meaning, 106, 109

Index

Heidegger on logotherapy and hermeneutics, 43
Husserl on logotherapy and hermeneutics, 47
Job and Frankl's existential vacuum, 58
Job and Frankl's will to meaning, 82
Job and the meaningful life, 59, 62
Job's monologue and existential self-analysis, 91
Job's response and the freedom to choose, 115
Job's turmoil in the existential vacuum, 66, 68
Job's wisdom poem and will to meaning, 84–85, 88
logotherapy and American psychology, 15
logotherapy and Job, 77
logotherapy and the friends of Job, 72–73
logotherapy and Viennese psychiatry, 12
nature of, 29–31
nature of divine communication, 95–96
place of past suffering, 97
spiritual unconscious, 34–36
statement of Job's problem, 7
Husserl, Edmund, 41, 46–48, 50–52
hymn, sapiential nature, 94, 99–102

Ilyich, Ivan, 19
imperative of logotherapy, categorical, 36, 91, 114
instinctual unconscious, 33, 115n57
intention, paradoxical, 37
The International Forum for Logotherapy, 17
The International Journal of Logotherapy and Existential Analysis, 17n94
International Journal of Psychoanalysis, 12
Ionesco, Eugene, 7
Isaiah, Book of, 68
Israel, 8, 58

J, Dr., 25
Jacob, 59
Jerusalem, Israel, 58
Jesus Christ, 18, 35
John, Gospel of, 21n115
Journal of Individual Psychology, 12–13
Jung, Carl, 3, 10n54, 13–14, 35

Kafka, Franz, 8
Klemm, David E., 1–2, 39–40, 43, 49, 54

La Chute (Camus), 104
LaCocque, André, 104
laws of dimensional ontology, 31–33
Leslie, Robert, 18–19
Leviathan, 67–68, 108–9, 115
Levinson, Jay, 17
life, meaningful
 Frankl and, 2, 11, 21, 26–27, 37, 45–46, 100, 115, 117
 Job and, 58–64, 121
logotherapy
 application of hermeneutics of, 55–56
 categorical imperative of, 36, 91, 114
 of Frankl, 10–19, 22–38
 and the friends of Job, 71–76
 and hermeneutics, 39–56
 and Job, 76–81
 of Job and his friends, 69–81
 summary of hermeneutics of, 53–54
 toward hermeneutics of, 20–21
Logotherapy and Existential Analysis: Proceedings of the Viktor Frankl Institute Vienna, Volume 1 (Batthyány), 17
Logotherapy in Action (Fabry et al.), 16
Logotherapy Textbook (Lukas), 16
Long, Jerry, 90
Lukas, Elisabeth, 16–17

Majdanek, 23
Man Decides for Himself: Viktor Frankl's Logotherapy and Existential Anthropology (Zamalieva), 17
Man's Search for Meaning (Frankl), 16

Index

Man's Search for Ultimate Meaning (Frankl), 4n23, 16
Maslow, Abraham, 15, 116n64
May, Rollo, 15
meaning
   life full of, 2, 11, 21, 26–27, 37, 45–46, 58–64, 100, 115, 117, 121
   of the moment, 28, 39, 68, 75–78, 84, 101, 114, 115n57, 120–22
   triad. *see* categorical values
   ultimate, 8, 28, 39, 56, 68, 71, 75–76, 84, 86, 101, 103–10, 112, 115, 117–23
   will to of Frankl, 9, 12, 15, 23, 26–29, 36, 45n39, 46, 55, 66, 121n5
   will to of Job, 10, 66–67, 82–102, 121
Michel, Walter L., 7, 111
moment, meaning of the
   eyes of a child, 120–22
   Frankl's assumptions and will to meaning, 28
   Job and Frankl's self-transcendence, 115n57
   Job and Frankl's will to meaning, 101
   Job's response and the freedom to choose, 114
   Job's turmoil in the existential vacuum, 68
   Job's wisdom poem and will to meaning, 84
   logotherapy and hermeneutics, 39
   logotherapy and Job, 77–78
   logotherapy and the friends of Job, 75–76
monologue
   of Elihu, 94–101
   of Job, 89–93
Moscow, Russia, 25
Moscow Institute of Psychoanalysis, 17

National Socialists, 27
nature hymn, sapiential, 94, 99–102
Nazis, 25, 27
Nemo, Philippe, 57, 65
neurosis, noogenic, 23, 64, 105, 121
Newell, B. Lynne, 110
Newsom, Carol A.
   Elihu's monologue, 94

God's speeches and ultimate meaning, 106, 108
Job and Frankl's existential vacuum, 57–58
Job and Frankl's self-transcendence, 103
Job and the meaningful life, 61–64
Job's monologue and existential self-analysis, 89, 92–93
Job's response and the freedom to choose, 111–12, 114–15
Job's turmoil in the existential vacuum, 64–66
Job's wisdom poem and will to meaning, 83, 86–88
logotherapy and Job, 76–78, 80
logotherapy and the friends of Job, 73, 75
logotherapy of Job and his friends, 70
place of past suffering, 98–99
sapiential nature hymn, 99–100
statement of Job's problem, 6–10
Noah, 59
noodynamics, 30, 33, 36
noogenic neurosis, 23, 64, 105, 121
noos, 29

On the Theory and Therapy of Mental Disorders (Frankl), 16
ontology, dimensional, 29–33, 30, 47, 60
Ophir, 82

paradox of suffering, terrible, 1–21
paradoxical intention, 37
past suffering, place of, 82, 96–99
person, human
   clinical applications of logotherapy, 36–37
   common roots of logotherapy and hermeneutics, 43
   existential vacuum, 23
   Frankl's answer to Jung, 13
   Frankl's assumptions and will to meaning, 26–27
   God's speeches and ultimate meaning, 106, 109

Index

Heidegger on logotherapy and hermeneutics, 43
Husserl on logotherapy and hermeneutics, 47
Job and Frankl's existential vacuum, 58
Job and Frankl's will to meaning, 82
Job and the meaningful life, 59, 62
Job's monologue and existential self-analysis, 91
Job's response and the freedom to choose, 115
Job's turmoil in the existential vacuum, 66, 68
Job's wisdom poem and will to meaning, 84–85, 88
logotherapy and American psychology, 15
logotherapy and Job, 77
logotherapy and the friends of Job, 72–73
logotherapy and Viennese psychiatry, 12
nature of, 29–31
nature of divine communication, 95–96
place of past suffering, 97
spiritual unconscious, 34–36
statement of Job's problem, 7
place of past suffering, 82, 96–99
poem, Job's wisdom, 3, 9, 55, 83–90, 101
Polak, Paul, 119n2
Pope, Marvin, 75
problem, statement of Job's, 5–10
Proverbs, Book of, 88
Psalms, Book of, 68
psychiatry, logotherapy and Viennese, 11–13
psychology, logotherapy and American, 14–16
The Pursuit of Meaning (Fabry), 16

Qoheleth, 8, 123

religio, 33–35
response of Job to God, 110–15
Rice, George E., 17

Ricoeur, Paul, 2–3, 41, 50–54
Rogers, Carl, 15
roots of logotherapy and hermeneutics, common, 41–53
Russia, 25
Russian Federation, 17

Sadigh, Micah, 19, 123n14
Sahakian, William S., 16, 21
Salzburg, Austria, 101
San Quentin State Prison, 23, 123n14
sapiential nature hymn, 94, 99–102
Sartre, Jean-Paul, 84n11, 109n30
Saudi Arabia, 61
Saying Yes to Life in Spite of Everything: A Psychologist Experiences the Concentration Camp (Frankl), 113
Scheler, Max, 41, 47–48, 60, 85n15, 112–13
Scherer, Paul, 61
Schleiermacher, Friedrich, 42–43
Schwarz, Oswald, 13n71
Second Force psychology, 14
second law of dimensional ontology, 32–33, 33
self-analysis, Job's existential, 82, 89–93, 101, 121
self-distance, 36
self-transcendence
clinical applications of logotherapy, 37–38
eyes of a child, 120, 122
of Job and Frankl, 103–18
Job and Frankl's will to meaning, 102
logotherapy and American psychology, 15
sapiential nature hymn, 101
spiritual unconscious, 34
Shema Yisrael, 113
Sheol, 76
Sirach, 99
Society for Individual Psychology, 10, 12–13, 47
Soelle, Dorothee, 63
Sophia, 3
speeches, God's
about, 104–10

Index

speeches, God's *(continued)*
  application of a logotherapy hermeneutic, 55
  Elihu's monologue, 94
  eyes of a child, 120
  Job and Frankl's self-transcendence, 103, 117
  Job's response and the freedom to choose, 111–12
  logotherapy and the friends of Job, 75n88
  statement of Job's problem, 8
  terrible paradox of suffering, 1
  and ultimate meaning, 104–10
Spiegelberg, Herbert, 45–46
spiritual unconscious, 13–14, 33–36, 102, 107, 110
SS, 28
statement of Job's problem, 5–10
Steinhof, 25, 93
suffering
  place of past, 82, 96–99
  terrible paradox of, 1–21
summary of a logotherapy hermeneutic, 53–54
Synchronization in Buchenwald, 17

Ten Commandments, 27–28
Terrien, Samuel, 61
Thayer, Joseph H., 21n115
Theresienstadt, 11–12
Third Force psychology, 14
today, logotherapy, 16–19
Tolstoy, Leo, 19, 24
tragic triad, 26, 72n72, 114, 123
transcendent unconscious, 34
Treblinka, 23
triad
  meaning. *see* categorical values
  tragic, 26, 72n72, 114, 123
Trilogy (Beckett), 104
The Triumph of Impotence: Job and the Tradition of the Absurd (Cox), 7
Turkheim, Germany, 11
turmoil of Job
  about, 64–68
  application of a logotherapy hermeneutic, 55

eyes of a child, 121
God's speeches and ultimate meaning, 105–7
Job and Frankl's existential vacuum, 57, 81
Job and Frankl's self-transcendence, 117n66
Job's monologue and existential self-analysis, 89
logotherapy and Job, 77, 80
logotherapy and the friends of Job, 73
logotherapy of Job and his friends, 69–70

ultimate meaning
  about, 104–10
  application of a logotherapy hermeneutic, 56
  eyes of a child, 119–23
  Frankl's assumptions and will to meaning, 28
  Job and Frankl's self-transcendence, 103, 117–18
  Job and Frankl's will to meaning, 101
  Job's response and the freedom to choose, 112, 115
  Job's turmoil in the existential vacuum, 68
  Job's wisdom poem and will to meaning, 84, 86
  logotherapy and hermeneutics, 39
  logotherapy and the friends of Job, 75–76
  logotherapy of Job and his friends, 71
  statement of Job's problem, 8
unconscious
  instinctual, 33, 115n57
  spiritual, 13–14, 33–36, 102, 107, 110
  transcendent, 34

vacuum, existential
  of Frankl, 23–25, 55, 120, 123n14
  of Job, 57–81, 105–6, 108, 121–22
values

attitudinal, 25–26, 55, 59–62, 64, 66–67, 71, 73, 76–77, 79, 81–82, 91, 93, 113, 117, 120–22
categorical, 25–26, 28, 47, 55, 59, 75–76, 82, 85n15, 91–92, 113–15, 117, 120
creative, 25–26, 55, 57, 59–62, 65, 67, 71, 73, 76–77, 79–82, 84, 91, 93, 113, 117, 120–21
experiential, 25–26, 55, 57, 59–62, 65, 67, 71, 73, 76–77, 79–82, 90–91, 93, 102, 113, 116–17, 120–21
Vesely, Franz, 119n2
Vesely-Frankl, Gabrielle, 119n2
Vienna, Austria, 4, 25, 27
Viennese psychiatry, logotherapy and, 11–13
Viktor Frankl Archives, 5n23
Viktor Frankl Institute of Logotherapy (United States), 4, 15–17
Viktor Frankl Institute (Vienna), 4, 5n23, 17n94

Viktor Frankl's Logotherapy (Graber), 17

Washburn, Michael, 15
Welter, Paul, 17
Westphal, Merold, 41–42, 50, 54
will
  freedom of the, 26, 36, 46
  to meaning of Frankl, 9, 12, 15, 23, 26–29, 36, 45n39, 46, 55, 66, 121n5
  to meaning of Job, 10, 66–67, 82–102, 121
The Will to Meaning (Frankl), 4–5nn23–24, 16
wisdom poem, Job's, 3, 9, 55, 83–90, 101
World War II, 27

Yalom, Irvin, 15

Zamalieva, Snezhana, 17
Zophar, 69–70, 75–76